THE KING'S FLYSWATTER

DANA ROBINSON

This publication is designed to provide accurate and authoritative information on the subjects addressed herein. However, neither the author, publisher nor their affiliates, officers, directors, subsidiaries and assigns are providing or rendering legal, accounting, or other professional services herein. If you need legal, accounting or other professional advice, you must seek your own professional and not look to this book as a substitute for such services. Some stories and names have been intentionally changed to preserve privacy and some creative liberties are taken in the interest of efficiency, but are immaterial in the opinion of the author.

Dana Robinson is a licensed attorney in California and Nevada, and a licensed real estate broker in California. However, his writing in this and other books and in other media is not intended as legal or real estate advice. Such advice should be specifically tailored to suit your needs. Books that provide self-help, including this one, are not a replacement or substitute for professional advice, which must be given considering your specific needs.

This book does not contain medical, psychological, or health advice. It provides information for general and educational purposes only.

The examples, stories and individuals discussed in this book are, in some instances, fictionalized or anonymized for the protection of the privacy of the individuals.

Published in the United States of America

Hardcover: 978-1-7322872-5-9
Paperback: 978-1-7322872-6-6
eBook: 978-1-7322872-7-3
Audiobook: 978-1-7322872-8-0

Cover design by: Printopya
Interior design by: Printopya
Illustrations by: Kok Kar Ying
Author photo by: Flavio Scorsato

Published by Opt Out Media
PO Box 1416, La Jolla, CA 92038
www.danarobinson.com

To my friend,

Joshua Mitchell

CONTENTS

FOREWORD
BY PAT FLYNN

2008 was not an easy year for me. After five years of studying at one of the top architecture schools in the country and then landing my dream job at a highly-rated firm, I was let go. Just as things were starting to get good, shortly after being promoted, my dream was now suddenly whisked away. Riding the train home that night, I worried about my future. Little did I know this early ending was the start of something incredible.

While working as an architect, I'd launched a website called GreenExamAcademy.com with the goal of sharing my notes for an exam a lot of my peers were taking. To be honest, it was a lazy way of saving myself unnecessary work. Instead of lugging around a few tons of textbooks with me everywhere I went (especially when traveling), I could consult my own notes online and prepare whenever I had a few minutes to spare. Eventually, I did pass, moved up in the company, and then forgot all about the website.

After I was laid off and was trying to figure out what to do next, I remembered the site. To my surprise, when I checked back in on it, I saw that tens of thousands of people had visited it in the previous six months. Obviously, I was aware it was publicly available to anyone who wanted to use the notes to study, but I had no idea it had reached that many people.

And that gave me an idea.

After being told I was being downsized, I had a few months to prepare before officially being out of work. During this time, I had a decision to make. Would I try to find another job at another firm in an already questionable market? Or would I pivot to something new? At this point, I'd invested eight years of schooling and professional experience into architecture, so it made sense to keep going in that direction. But there was something else gnawing at me. Something I can only describe as the entrepreneurial itch.

In the years since graduating college and becoming an architect, I'd begun listening to podcasts and reading blogs about online marketing and business. It fascinated me. Just the year before getting laid off, Tim Ferriss's phenomenal bestseller *The Four Hour Workweek* had come out, and everyone was talking about it. In those days, everywhere you looked someone was talking about outsourcing and lifestyle design and the Pareto Principle. And it was all seemingly made possible by entrepreneurship.

I had never started a business before but was curious to see if I had what it took. At the time, I'd just proposed to my girlfriend (now wife), and we were talking about starting a family. Before getting married and becoming a dad, though, I wanted the stability of a good job. But traditional employment no longer seemed so secure. What I really longed for was a steady income stream with the most freedom possible. Was that even a thing?

Little did I know, hidden in years of experience as an architect and student, was the beginning of a new kind of education, one where I could leverage what I'd done in one industry to make a much bigger move in another.

In architecture school, I'd learned mostly abstract concepts. School was useful but nowhere near as practical as what those first few months on the job had to teach me. After three years of working at the firm, however, all my hard work seemed to be for nothing. But was it? I'd learned a lot in a short time, including how to quickly master new skills, how to problem-solve on the fly, and how to lead. Maybe these skills were useful elsewhere, perhaps even in a job I could create for myself. All I needed to know was where to apply them.

The final few months of working as an architect, I turned that same level of studiousness I had applied to my exams to learning everything I could about online marketing. Devouring every podcast I could get my hands on, I went back to school, so to speak, and gave myself the best education possible—in a relatively short time. I didn't just memorize ideas and answers, though; I listened to what other people had done and applied those same lessons and principles to my own situation.

Retooling my old study notes website into a resource for others, I began selling study guides and practice exams online, following the eBook craze of the time. And in less than a year, I had increased my income by 250%. After that, there was no turning back. I was all in on entrepreneurship, and the rest—as they say—is history.

By taking the lessons I'd learned from a day job and a handful of online teachers, I was able to build a life for myself and my family that gave us the ultimate freedom. I didn't do this by "burning the boats" or going "all in" without consideration of the consequences. Instead, I became what Dana Robinson calls a "flyswatter"—someone who takes a lowly position on purpose so they can learn the tricks of a new trade.

To be fair, I didn't choose this but was forced into it by getting laid off. Nonetheless, by following in the footsteps of a handful of mentors who had gone before me, I was able to leverage my skills as an architect and turn them into something far more useful and profitable. By solving a simple problem for myself and then sharing the solution with others, I was able to accomplish my dream of going to work for myself. Not because I took a huge risk, but because "flyswatting" always works when you know how it works.

Sure, I could have stubbornly stuck to architecture. But there was something attractive about the entrepreneurial lifestyle, something I wanted. Pursuing a new career essentially meant starting over, but my instincts told me it would be worth it. I'm glad to say that bet paid off. But to be honest, it wasn't that risky. It was just about seeing an opportunity and using the skills I'd already developed, then applying them to a new outlet.

In an age when everyone is telling you to go big or go home, the truth is there is a smarter way to create the freedom you crave. You don't have to mortgage everything you hold dear for the possibility of success. You can use the experience and knowledge you've already acquired, while employing the multitude of teachers around you to fill the gaps.

Becoming an entrepreneur is not some special achievement reserved for the elite. Anyone can do it, so long as they're willing to swat some flies. It may not happen as quickly as you'd like, but I promise the effects will be longer-lasting than the alternative. It has been fifteen years since that fateful day I was laid off, catapulting me into a surprise career as a digital entrepreneur, online teacher, and business advisor. And I couldn't be happier.

The success that many of my peers and I have experienced is due to a concept I wish more people understood, which Dana so smartly unpacks in this book. Flyswatting is not necessarily glamorous, but when you put yourself in the position of humble learner, you gain an education no school could ever offer. And when you know what to do with that, the rewards are unimaginable.

There's a whole world of possibility awaiting you, hidden

in the work that no one wants to do. And you don't have to wait for something terrible to happen, as I did, so that you can start creating the freedom you want. Choose to be a fly-swatter—today. It's the best way to get ahead.

Don't believe me? That's okay. I didn't, either. That's why I'm glad this book exists. Keep reading. Start swatting. See you on the other side.

CAST OF CHARACTERS

Anki: Chief cook in the palace, an ally of Ubar

Anu: God of the Sky

Bashaa: Ubar's former employer, benefactor and business partner, brother of Yahatti

Elishu: The foremost cattle trader in Namir

Kuri: A former flyswatter and career servant at the palace, close friend of Rihat

Lebashi: A flyswatter to the king who was placed under Ubar's authority

Rihat: Trainer of royal flyswatters who became chief steward, an enemy of Ubar

Sabium: Emperor of Babylon, the grandson of Tattannu and son of Abdili

Sargon: King of Akkadia, which controlled the areas around Namir

Tattannu: First great King of Namir, said to be the son of Anu, God of the Sky

Ubar: An orphaned servant boy who became the king's flyswatter

Yahatti: King Tattannu's chief steward and trusted advisor, brother of Bashaa

PREFACE

This is a book about getting ahead at work and in life. It is intended for anyone who has a desire to find more fulfilling work, a greater sense of freedom, and a higher level of financial success than their current job affords.

If you hate your job and can't bear the idea of walking into work for even one more day, this book is for you. If you dream of starting your own business, being your own boss, and taking control of your financial future but aren't sure how, this book is for you. If you've been putting off your life's great adventure because you don't feel smart enough or talented enough, this book is for you.

This is the story of how I made the leap from being an employee to being an entrepreneur. It involves a great deal of personal growth, learning, skill development, networking, and planning. And it includes a significant tolerance for risk.

But I assure you it is a pathway you can follow too, no matter what you dream of doing.

The premise of this book is a simple, but often overlooked, truth: You are responsible for you. The best way to succeed in business, or anywhere, is to shed your sense of entitlement, stop looking for someone else to provide opportunities and rewards, quit wishing on a star, and chart your own pathway to success. To do that, you'll need to make a significant shift in your thinking. You will need to see yourself not as an expert, but as a learner; not as entitled to respect, but as willing to take on humble roles. Look at every job you have as an opportunity to learn. Master your job, then master your boss's job, then master everything else you can. Work hard. Make yourself valuable. Then leverage that knowledge and experience to gain a promotion, find a new job, or even start a venture of your own. No one else—not your boss, not senior management, not the government, not your parents—is responsible for your success and wellbeing. You are responsible for you.

That message is somewhat countercultural today. Many people enter the workforce with a sense of entitlement, believing they are owed a certain level of income or number of perks. It has almost become fashionable for people to make demands from employers based on their education, sense of self-worth, or notion of "rights" before contributing a single day's effort. Employers are increasingly seen as benefactors, responsible for ensuring every aspect of an employee's welfare.

Certainly the provision of fair wages and safe working conditions is a fundamental responsibility for any employer. Yet it's misguided and counterproductive to take a paternalistic view of employment. In reality, every one of us is self-employed. Wherever you are and whatever you're doing, you are responsible for ensuring your own success. You are self-employed. All of us are, even though we may appear to be working for an employer. Making demands and insisting on entitlements are short-term strategies. They make your job a little better today, but do nothing to prepare you for long-term success. We all encounter some employment inequities that need to be corrected, and we're right to demand action. Yet in the long term, you, not your employer, are responsible for your success.

To convey this concept fully and make it, hopefully, more entertaining, I've woven it into a parable. This book is also a story—or rather, two stories. The first is a tale of personal success. It's the story of a young man named Ubar, who lived thousands of years ago in the ancient kingdom of Babylon. Ubar was a servant with one of the lowliest of all jobs: flyswatting. As you follow Ubar's life story, the success pathway I'm advocating will become clear. I call it "the Way of the Flyswatter."

The second story is my own. In alternating chapters you will read the story of Ubar, the young flyswatter, and of actual budding entrepreneurs. The real-life portions of the book explain the concepts hidden in the parable and demonstrate how they have worked for me and in the lives of others. I've been following the Way of the Flyswatter all my adult life, and it's brought a great deal of satisfaction and wealth.

Here's my message to you in a nutshell: You don't need to win the lottery to get out of the situation you are in. You don't need a stroke of genius, or to make a lucky investment. And you certainly don't need to quit your job in the blind faith that something better will come along. You have, right now, the starting point for the life you truly want. It is the job you already have.

Now turn the page, and let me prove that to you.

I

THE ORPHAN

A thousand years before Nebuchadnezzar II reigned over the kingdom of Babylon, there was a wise king who ruled a prosperous city between the rivers. King Tattannu was said to be the son of Anu, God of the Sky. Tattannu had ruled Namir since he was very young, during the time Sargon and the Akkadians controlled all of Sumeria.

Namir had prospered under King Tattannu's rule for decades, and during this time commerce with other cities flourished. The city of Namir was known for justice, largely because Tattannu sat as judge almost daily to hear his subjects' disputes and make rulings.

There was very little poverty in Namir, but its citizens included a lot of hardworking immigrants who lived on subsistence labor. Many were indentured servants earning their right to citizenship by working for seven years for Namir's farmers, miners, and builders. With poverty comes sickness and untimely death, and it was the untimely death of his mother that made an orphan of a young boy named Ubar.

Ubar's father had died in battle years before, defending his home city far away. Ubar's mother brought him to Namir where she got a job washing linens and found a room for them both. When his mother died, Ubar was left completely alone at the age of eleven.

Ubar's mother had worked for a wealthy businessman named Bashaa. He was kind enough, but not at all pleased to be responsible for an eleven-year-old boy. At his young age, Ubar would not make a good laborer, and the master did not want to feed and house the child until he could make himself useful in the fields.

Ubar, though young, was not unaware of his predicament. He understood that his best hope was to further Bashaa's interests any way he could. So Ubar looked for small opportunities to be of service. When the cook served the master's meals, Ubar followed along, clearing the plates and sweeping up afterward. When the chief steward received supplies for the master's estate, Ubar memorized where each item was stored and quickly put them in place.

Though he knew his place in Bashaa's household was a precarious one, Ubar looked on each day as an opportunity to help—both Bashaa and himself. Still, Bashaa paid him no notice.

One day Bashaa's brother Yahatti came for a visit. Yahatti

was a wise and important man. He served as chief steward for King Tattannu. While the brothers enjoyed a meal together, Ubar, as usual, helped to serve food and clean up.

Although Bashaa was one of the more prosperous men in Namir, he lamented his situation to his brother.

"The grain market has fallen to pieces," he complained. "I have no workers to gather the harvest. What's more, I'm saddled with this useless orphan to feed and clothe."

Yahatti regarded the boy with a discerning eye.

"Perhaps he could be a flyswatter for one of your foremen," he suggested. "That would be something."

Bashaa snorted in disgust.

"Not likely," he said. "All he does is pick up scraps, and I have dogs for that."

Yahatti wondered if his brother was perhaps exaggerating the child's incompetence.

"May I speak with the boy?" he asked, not revealing that he already had work in mind for him.

"Of course," replied Bashaa. "I hope you can find something for him and take him off my hands."

That evening, Bashaa sent for Ubar.

"Tomorrow morning you must go to the king's palace," he said. "My brother is chief steward. Go to the back of the palace and ask for Yahatti. He may have a place for you."

Ubar barely slept that night. Fears about what lay ahead danced through his mind. Was he being sold as a slave to the king? Would he ever return to Bashaa's house, the only home he had ever known? What if there was no place for him at the palace? Would he then be reduced to wander the streets and beg?

The first streams of morning light were enough to scatter Ubar's fear.

"This is dangerous," he concluded, "but it is also an opportunity. I have a home here and food to eat. But picking up scraps like a dog is no life for me. I will go to the palace, come what may."

When Ubar arrived at the servant's gate, he was taken to a small office where Yahatti's table stood covered in parchment. Polished stones decorated with carved characters lay atop the papers. A clay pitcher sat on his table. Yahatti poured water from it into a cup and handed it to Ubar.

"I am Yahatti, chief steward for King Tattannu. I am in charge of the many workers who serve the king's palace. I would like to offer you a job."

Ubar's eyes were wide with surprise.

"Yes please, sir."

Yahatti sat on a stool, one arm on his knee, the other stroking his beard. The young Ubar was very thin, and Yahatti could see that he was not capable of hard labor. Yet he saw eagerness in the boy's face.

"The work is lowly," Yahatti said. "Beyond that, there is little hope for promotion and the prospect of severe punishment for failure. Most servants avoid this assignment and leave it as quickly as they can. Yet it is one of the most important jobs in the palace."

Yahatti paused. He was thinking of the great

contradiction found in the task. It was truly one of the lowliest and dirtiest jobs in the palace, but by taking it on, no servant did more to assure the king's success.

"It is flyswatter to the king," Yahatti continued. "Your job would be to stand near the king each day as he holds court, swatting flies before they can land on his royal person."

Ubar blinked.

"This job is dirty and boring," Yahatti said. "Yet it allows the king to give his full attention to the kingdom."

Yahatti picked up a handle attached to a long tuft of horsetail hair. Yahatti swung it near Ubar's head, making the boy flinch. Yahatti laughed.

"I just saved you from a fly that was buzzing by your ear," he said. "Did you hear it?"

"Yes, sir. I heard the fly, and he is no longer. Thank you."

"Your job would be to do the same for our great king. You will ensure that no flies bother him while he sits in judgment of our citizens' disputes," said Yahatti.

He continued, "Do you see why this is an important job?"

Ubar thought about this for a moment and then replied, "Well, no great king should be bothered by such pests. I have seen the foremen in the fields and in the brick works. They have a servant doing this same thing. Of course the king is greater than such foremen. He also must be free of pests."

"Very good," said Yahatti. "And have you also seen what happens when a flyswatter fails at his task?"

"Yes," said Ubar hesitantly. "He is punished when a fly

lands on the foreman. And if the flyswatter strikes the foreman's skin, the flyswatter is beaten severely."

"It is indeed a thankless job with few rewards," said Yahatti. "Are you willing to do it?"

A pang of fear stabbed Ubar's chest. He could go back to Bashaa's house if he chose—that seemed safer. Yet it was also pointless. At best, he would scurry about the house picking up scraps until he was old enough to be sent to the fields or the mines. Swatting flies was certainly no better than being a house servant, and there was greater risk of punishment. Yet it was a position in the king's palace, no matter how lowly.

"Yes," said Ubar. "I will do it." He hesitated, unsure if he dared say more. At last he decided to risk a question. "If I may ask, sir. Why did you choose me?"

Yahatti's eyes twinkled. "Why you, Ubar?" he said with a smile. "Why not you?"

And so Ubar moved into the servants' quarters at the back of the palace, where he was fed with the lowest ranking servants and taught the rules. Yahatti handed Ubar over to an old man who, Ubar learned, had once been the king's flyswatter. While the old man was not feeble, he had become arthritic and could not spend his day swinging a swatter. He now trained new servants in the art of swatting flies. The old man's name was Rihat.

PRINCIPLE #1

WORK SUCKS, BUT YOU'RE NEVER STUCK.

Now let me tell you a story about my good friend Cory. It could be your story too, or the story of anyone who gets a job—maybe a job they are excited about or maybe just a job they need, but a job that they soon realize sucks.

Cory had what most people would consider a great job as a project manager for a large software development company. He spent a couple of years buying into the job and believing that it was going to help him achieve his personal and professional goals. Like most employees, Cory valued security, and his company provided that. He had stock options. He was making a decent salary with good benefits. Cory realized, however, he not only was dissatisfied with his job, he hated it. But it was just too much to walk away from. So he kept grinding it out year after year, always thinking there would be a big promotion just over the horizon that would finally bring a sense of satisfaction to his work.

The promotions, when they came, never seemed to solve his basic problem—finding meaning in a job he neither liked nor wanted. He held on for too long and hung his hopes on the stock options, which he assumed would make up for all of his misery. When the company sold, he imagined he would make at least a million dollars. He could then choose his own path, find the work he wanted to do, or maybe start a business.

Finally, it got to be too much. One day, after his usual sixty-minute commute to work, Cory walked up to the front door and stopped. He felt himself involuntarily freeze; he couldn't lift his arm. He later told me he just couldn't force himself to reach out and open the door. He even had a physical reaction to this panic—his vision blurry, his ears ringing.

Perhaps that has happened to you, albeit in a less dramatic fashion. I've heard similar stories from lots of people who woke up one day and realized the thought of going to the office made them physically ill. We all want to do something that brings meaning and satisfaction to our lives. But work? Trading your time for money? Doing things that seem pointless and boring day after day, year after year? Well, that just sucks.

That's why we've become experts in self-distraction. We cope with our work dissatisfaction through any means possible: indulging in social media for hours at a time, following sports, watching television—anything we can find to keep us from dealing with our unhappiness. Many self-medicate with alcohol or other drugs, blocking out the pain every weekend or even every day. Nearly all of us have lain awake at night rehearsing one of those Jerry Maguire speeches where we'll tell off the boss, declare our moral and professional freedom, and walk out in a righteous fury.

That's pretty much what Cory did. That crisis was the culmination of years of frustration. The last straw had been a company merger that reduced his stock options to almost nothing. Cory was filled with anger at the C-suite, now filled with ruthless managers who had turned the office into a sweatshop.

"I poured my life into that place," he later told me, "and I've got nothing."

Unsurprisingly, Cory turned on his heel, got in his car and drove home. He quit on the spot. No safety net. No plan. No future vision. All he wanted was to stop the pain, so that's what he did.

Many people feel the way Cory did. You may feel that way now. It's no fun to be stuck in a place that sucks the life out of you. I'll tell you more about how Cory's life turned out (he's an amazing success now). But it's not because of what he did that day. In fact, I'd like to catch your attention before you do what Cory did, before you get to the point where you reach the office and can't lift your hand to open the door.

Stop Looking for a Magic Bullet

You aren't alone if you feel like Cory. Most modern workers are moderately discontented with their situation. It's the zeitgeist of the middle-class workforce, from the blue collar tradesperson to the working rich. Millions of people feel the same pressure Cory felt. And every day, many of them take a blind leap in the hope that their next move—any move—will land them in a better place.

A recent news headline captures this dynamic perfectly: "Crypto crash FOMO." The article contains an all-too-familiar story of burnout and blind faith. "I missed the bus on Bitcoin," one investor says, "but now feel like my time has come. I have another 25 years of a boring 9-to-5 job, and I just want out. I sit here day after day, doing the same old drudgery, and I want to have some hope that I may have an exit strategy."[1]

One reason crypto gained popularity was that people saw it as a quick way to get out of the rat race. People jump at bubble-like opportunities because they feel desperate. Something, anything, has to be better than going to their job every day. So they buy a lottery ticket out of their moderate discontent. They believe the only way out is to go big or go home. They sink their savings into crypto, launch an improbable business scheme from their garage, or just quit and hope a golden opportunity will magically present itself.

That seldom works out. In my experience, both as an entrepreneur and as a coach and counselor to thousands of people making the switch from employment to ownership, instant success is rare. Most of the Corys in the world wind up back at another job they don't love. Here's the secret no one talks about: Most successful entrepreneurs got to where they are by doing something at their job that gave them an edge. Then they leveraged that to become self-employed.

Long before you reach that point, I'd like to show you how the job you have, no matter how frustrating or tedious it may be, can actually be your ticket out.

Best/Worst Job Ever

I learned that lesson a number of years ago while making a start in the real estate business. Many people get into real estate because it seems like a good way to make money quickly. Not long ago, weekend workshops on how to make your first million in the housing market were quite common. Today, flipping properties is seen as a rapid pathway to success. Something about this business taps into the feeling we all seem to have: we deserve to get rich without much effort. It may work out that way for some, but the one sure way to find success in real estate, or in any industry, is to start at the beginning and learn the business from bottom to top. That's exactly what I did.

When I was accepted into law school, I needed a job to pay rent on an apartment so I could help provide for my wife and two-year-old daughter. I landed a job that would provide both income and housing. My wife and I shared duties as the on-site property managers of a small apartment building. It was located at the beach, which was a really big win. However, in order to make enough money, my wife and I would have to clean the apartments that were rented out to vacationers. Over the span of three years, my wife and I cleaned a *lot* of apartments.

The entire experience was an insight into how thoughtless people can be. We changed sheets, did laundry, swept and mopped, cleaned the dishes and kitchens, and cleaned the toilets. As it happened, most of the toilet cleaning landed on me. I had some expertise in this department because I had a high-school job as a lowly worker at a gas station. I had cleaned the gas station bathroom hundreds of times. Toilet cleaning is the worst job I've had. But it had to be done. And I had bills to pay. So I pulled on yellow rubber gloves, covered the bowl with scrubbing bubbles and did a job most people would find too disgusting to take on.

Here's the thing: I never saw myself as a toilet cleaner, even though I did it nearly every day. I saw myself as a future real estate entrepreneur, learning the basics of managing a successful vacation rental operation. Vacation renters take a beach apartment for a week and pay a premium for the privilege of living in an apartment rather than a hotel room. The business behind the dirty toilets was very profitable. I quickly realized that this was a business I'd never known and would probably never have learned if I hadn't taken the job of property manager. My wife and I learned everything we could about vacation rentals, but cleaning toilets was part of the price to learn the business.

A few years later, I was a young lawyer with a paycheck and had no further need to clean bathrooms. But the lessons I'd learned as chief toilet cleaner began to pay off. I bought a beach condo and turned it into a vacation rental that paid for itself and made monthly income. I would later sell that condo for double what I'd paid. We bought a second condo, which made us hundreds of thousands of dollars in income, as well as hundreds of thousands more when we sold it. We also used our acumen to buy a vacation rental management business from a man who was retiring. We grew that business fourfold in four years and sold it for substantially more than we'd paid for it. And that was after making a six-figure annual income from it.

Over the past twenty years we have owned, grown, and sold three property management companies. The cumulative income from our real estate ventures is in the millions. We would have made none of that money if we'd demanded the apartment owners hire a housekeeping service so we wouldn't have to do the work we saw as beneath us. In reality, toilet cleaning wasn't a job for me. It was an opportunity to learn how the rental business really worked.

You have that same opportunity right now, regardless of the situation you're in. You can choose to see yourself as a drone stuck in a dead-end job, or you can view yourself as a future entrepreneur who has been given the gift of on-the-job training; even if your particular "on-the-job training" sucks like mine did.

You Don't Need a Job

Let's admit the obvious: work sucks. It sucks for everybody. So if your job sucks, that's par for the course. This isn't what most people want to hear. We've been raised to believe that going to college, earning a degree, then getting a good job is a no-fail pathway to a good income and a meaningful life. We don't want to believe that work is mostly drudgery and seldom leaves us with a sense of fulfillment. Yet anyone who has had a job for more than a couple of years has already come to the conclusion that we've been fooled with the idea that having a good job will bring us the American Dream.

Companies push that message—get a good education, get a good job, work hard, get promoted—because they need human capital to make a profit. Colleges feed the same propaganda. Rather than simply providing a liberal education that builds inquiring minds that can speak languages, think creatively, and apply the wisdom of history and science to the world, colleges recruit students on the idea of getting trained for a career. Even public elementary and secondary schools, as Seth Godin[2] has pointed out, were created as human capital factories. Their purpose was to supply workers for the industrial economy.

Now let's state something that's not so obvious: you don't need a job. We have jobs because the world tells us we need jobs. Kings need flyswatters—also cooks, accountants, servants, architects, and advisors. However, kings do not have jobs in the traditional sense. They don't work in the way their subjects do, selling their labor in exchange for money. A king's work is applying wisdom to problem-solving, making decisions, directing the effort of others, exercising foresight. These things are not labor in the traditional sense; they are activities of the mind. So the path out of "work" and into a more satisfying use of our time and energy is also a path of the mind. It is a pathway that leads away from being a tool for someone else's profit to using our skills and abilities to profit ourselves.

When a CEO or business leader says, "We all need to work hard," it's total bullshit. We really don't have to perform boring, seemingly meaningless tasks all day long in order to survive, not if we don't want to. Kings don't do that. Neither do CEOs, entrepreneurs, and small business owners. But you can't just snap your fingers and go from employee to business owner.

Most of us don't begin life as kings—or CEOs or business

owners. We begin somewhere closer to where Ubar started, at the bottom of the economic ladder with what seems to be extremely limited options. Ubar quickly realized he had very little choice about the type of work he did. He could pick up table scraps, or he could swat flies. Both were menial and thankless jobs. But Ubar had already decided that he, not Bashaa nor even Yahatti, would determine his future. He was responsible for himself, the work he did, and the choices he made. So Ubar went to work in the palace, not for the job but for the opportunity. In the king's service, Ubar knew he would have a far greater chance of improving his situation; even doing the worst job ever.

You Are Not Stuck

Yes, work sucks. But every job, no matter how distasteful, provides an opportunity for personal growth. Toilet cleaning was an opportunity for me to learn about real estate, about people, and about all the labor that goes into the rental business. That job was a gift. The same is true for you, no matter what role or industry you're working in. You have an opportunity to learn your job, the rudiments of your industry, and your boss's job. You have a chance to observe people and see how they go about their work—to see what makes them valuable employees or not.

When you reach the point my friend Cory did, believing that you simply can't stand the drudgery and pointlessness for one more day, remember this. *You are not stuck.* You do have options. That job does not define you, and it certainly has no claim on your life. Your employer is not using you; don't frame your current career as a victim. You are using your job as a platform for learning and personal growth. Where you are now is merely the starting point for your future. You have the power to move from employee to entrepreneur. In fact, you are already self-employed. You are the CEO and general manager of you.

That's the first thing you should take on board from the story of Ubar the flyswatter. He took responsibility for himself. He had a terrible job. He received room and board in exchange for doing menial tasks. Yet he spent no time complaining about the situation. Ubar realized that creating a better future for himself was entirely up to him. He knew he couldn't count on Bashaa, his employer, to provide training and a career path. Whatever would become of Ubar was up to Ubar, and he knew that. So he did the one thing he could control, even as a servant with no education and obvious skills: he worked hard. He realized if he could make himself valuable to an employer, that would probably create opportunities in the future. And that's exactly what happened.

The first thing you'll need to do to move from employee to entrepreneur is to take responsibility for yourself. Your education, your career training, your skill development, your advancement or promotion—these things are not up to your boss. They are up to you. You are not stuck in your dead-end job. You have the power to create a better future for yourself.

As we continue to follow Ubar's story, I'll share more stories of my own that show the way in which his experience, though fictionalized, is very much true to life. By the end of this book, you should be ready to take real steps toward breaking free of a job you don't like and forging your own path through your job and, probably, out of it.

You are not as stuck as you may feel right now. You can make a big career change if you understand that you have agency. You control what's next. So relax. Don't panic. Start to see your current job not as the ball-and-chain you must have for a secure life, but as the gateway to something better.

You will learn to leverage your current position to reach your next one. You'll become empowered to move up, over, or even out, like I did when I left my comfy job as an attorney to become an entrepreneur.

How do you do that?

Let's see how Ubar did and then I'll share my own story.

Flyswatting in Action

Work sucks, but you are never stuck. Don't disparage the present when it affords you the next step to your future.

The first step to self-employment is to change your attitude, not your situation. Think differently, and you'll act differently. And as you act differently, your life will slowly change.

Taking personal responsibility empowers personal change. And personal change is what we all want.

II

THE ETHICAL THIEF

Each day after breakfast, Ubar was tutored on the art of swatting flies by the previous servant Rihat. To do this, a different servant was forced to sit in a chair, pretending to be the King. Rihat drew the cloth back from the windows, allowing flies to enter freely, then charged Ubar not to let a single one land on the servant. The hapless minion was asked to sit still while Ubar swung a horsetail whisk within inches of his face. Sometimes Ubar struck the fly, sometimes he missed, and occasionally the whisk snapped at the servant's face or neck, provoking a loud cry. Rihat was wrathful against Ubar for his failures, telling him he would not ever survive as a flyswatter.

Ubar was kind; he made friends with his victims and he apologized profusely when he made a wrong move. Sometimes the other servants and Ubar would end up laughing hard. Rihat would take a serious tone and remind Ubar that the king hadn't been touched by a single horsehair for as long as Rihat could remember.

"We love our king, and he is a God. We do not let the flies touch him, nor do we let him feel the source of our vengeance on the flies," he said. "We bring tranquility to our king from behind him, and we are never to be noticed. We are invisible. There is no room for error."

Ubar sensed an air of desperation in Rihat's words. No room for error. There would be order in the king's palace, Rihat would make sure of that. Ubar understood this and took his training seriously. In the evenings, he practiced on his own. Ubar would set a grain of rice on a small patch of silk, then aim to move the rice without disturbing the fabric.

It was weeks before he was confident he could avoid contact. Rihat began taking Ubar and the extra servant near the kitchen so there would be more flies around. This was unfortunate for the servants, who fell victim to the nuisance of flies and Ubar's failure to avoid delivering blows to their necks, ears, and faces. It was lucky Ubar had shown himself to be authentic and kind, and now had friendship and trust with his practice subjects, as they forgave him quickly.

After a few months, Rihat called Ubar back to the practice room. Ubar was surprised to find Yahatti, the chief steward, standing there as well.

"Rihat tells me you have done well in your training," Yahatti said.

Ubar smiled and glanced at Rihat, whose face showed neither approval nor admiration.

"The boy has passed each test," Rihat said grudgingly. "He is ready to enter service." Turning to Ubar, he went on, "If you continue to be diligent and do your work well, you will have a long career in service to the king. If you do not, you will be cast out."

Ubar tried to suppress a smile. At last, he had found a secure place for himself.

"You will eventually earn larger quarters, more privileges, and even a pension from the king when you are too old to swat flies," Rihat continued sternly. "Follow the rules, do your job, and you may have a good life."

"I am eager to begin," Ubar responded.

"Good," said Yahatti. "Because tomorrow you will be tested by Kuri, the king's chief flyswatter. If you pass the test, you will take his place and serve the king as he sits in judgment for our citizens."

"Me?" Ubar asked. "On my first day, I will be the king's chief flyswatter?"

"Yes," Yahatti said. "You have proven your skill. Kuri must return to his duties as chief steward for the queen. Tomorrow, he will make sure you are entirely ready for this responsibility. I suggest you get a good night's sleep."

Old Rihat turned and left the room. Yahatti couldn't resist giving Ubar a pat on the shoulder.

"Well done, my son," he said.

The next day, Ubar returned to the practice room where Yahatti and Kuri stood waiting. In the chair was a servant to play the role of the king. Other servants stood outside, each representing a petitioner to the king. For ten hours, Ubar stood by the "king's" side, moving from right to left, swatting fly after fly. No flies landed on the servant's face—or even came close. The lash never brushed the servant's cheek.

"This one is very good," Kuri said. "You see how he is able to use the whisk with both hands?"

"Yes." Yahatti smiled in approval. "That cannot be taught. It is a natural talent."

At last, Kuri said, "Enough. He has passed the test. I pronounce him ready to enter the king's service."

"Congratulations, my boy," Yahatti said. "You have completed the first part of your training."

Ubar was too tired to respond. He bowed low, then gratefully retreated to the servant's hall.

That night Ubar had a small celebration with the servants who had helped him along the way. Each one congratulated him on his promotion. Ubar felt a sense of pride. Now barely twelve years old, he would stand in the king's presence every day, doing what he knew was a highly important task.

After a while, old Rihat approached the table of junior servants and congratulated Ubar.

"You have done well," he said. "Now remember your place. Respect your elders, and do as you are told. Better to be a lowly flyswatter than to live on the street."

And so Ubar took up his duties in the court of King Tattannu. Day by day, he stood behind the king, guarding against any fly that should dare to disturb the great man's concentration. Ubar learned to block out all other activities, sounds, and people to become one with the whisk. Not one fly landed on the king, who seemed completely unaware of Ubar's presence.

Day by day, the king sat in judgment, listening to squabbles between citizens. A fight over land. A controversy over an unpaid bill. An allegation of imbalanced weights and measures. To King Tattannu, the success of his reign depended on the success of his subjects, and his role as judge was the best way to keep commercial activity flowing.

It was also a way to show his strength as a leader. King Tattannu's impartiality and fairness became a theme for the entire city state. He was keenly focused during each hearing and learned a lot about his citizens. Over the years, he became an expert in humans. Their strength and their pettiness. Their passion and their pride. Their ability to walk with integrity and their capacity for untruth. He listened, asked a few questions to clarify, and then ruled with expert efficiency.

One by one, the years went by. Tattannu held court for four hours each afternoon. And for four hours, Ubar stood faithfully by his side. No flies landed on the king. Ubar had learned to enter a meditative state while working, taking into account only the flies and his whisk. His job became predictable and his personal life steady.

Evenings were spent with other staff, dining, playing games, and chatting. Rihat and Kuri spoke much about their jobs as flymasters. They were proud men who had done well. They often encouraged Ubar to stay focused on his job and not get distracted, so he could eventually be like them: secure in their station, their job, and their future. Ubar nodded and did not question that this was also his path. He observed the other servants who also seemed content in their jobs, well fed, happy, and secure. They did not aspire to greater wealth, nor did Ubar.

Ubar had a subtle sense that the job he was doing was almost too easy. It was becoming mundane. He saw that there was neither a path up nor anything different he could do. Given that his mentors had spent their entire careers doing the same thing, he began to despair. He did not feel he was above this job, but the thought of doing it for thirty more years gave him a knot in his stomach. He occasionally contemplated what life would be like out of the palace, and questioned his future. Yet, he continued to do his job with expert precision.

When Ubar turned sixteen, Yahatti called him aside.

"It's time for the second part of your training," he said.

"The second part?" Ubar was puzzled.

"Sit," Yahatti said. "We will discuss your work."

Yahatti asked Ubar about his work. Ubar talked excitedly about his knowledge and skill.

"What do you observe about the flies?" Yahatti asked.

"They return to the same place repeatedly," Ubar replied.

"What else," Yahatti continued.

"If they survive the touch of the whisk, they do not return to the same place I struck them. They seem to have memory."

"And?" inquired Yahatti.

"I can judge their movements based on my observations," responded Ubar.

"You are now one with the fly," laughed Yahatti. He continued in a more serious tone. "Do you remember what old Rihat said to you on the day you were promoted four years ago?"

"I do," said Ubar. "He said if I do my work well I will have a good life."

"Is that all?"

"Well, he also said that it would be a great blessing to the kingdom if I were to remain a flyswatter for life."

"Do you believe that?" Yahatti asked.

"I suppose. I know I am doing important work for the king. I enable him to make wise judgments for our people."

"That is true," Yahatti said. "But I think there is a greater blessing you might contribute."

"Me?" Ubar asked hesitantly. "I have wondered if I can do this job for my entire life, sir. But I am ashamed of feeling that way."

Yahatti laughed and said, "You feel the way anyone with your intelligence should feel. And that is why I have brought you here for this discussion.

"Tomorrow, I'd like you to try something that may be

very challenging," he went on. "Are you willing to try a little experiment?"

Ubar eagerly responded, "Yes, sir. Anything you wish."

"I would like you to listen keenly to the cases the king hears." Yahatti paused. "I know it is difficult to do anything else while swatting flies. But I believe you have the skill. You must continue to do your job to perfection. But you must also learn to tune your ears and mind to the cases and the king's rulings."

Ubar raised his brow and thought for a moment.

"Wouldn't it be dangerous to do two things at once? My job is to swat flies. If I fail, I'll be punished severely."

"Yes, you are correct. It is a dangerous proposition. I would not ask anyone else to do this except you because no one I have ever met seems capable."

Ubar remained unconvinced.

"I do not think it is my business to hear such things, nor is it useful. My place is to swat flies. I have no right to listen to the king's wisdom."

"Is it thievery to take what is freely available to all?" Yahatti smiled. "The king pronounces judgments for the good of the kingdom. Is it wrong for a citizen to learn the law?"

After a longer silence, Ubar said, "I agree. It is my duty to do my work. It is not a disservice to the king to do more than my work. I can learn from the king while serving him."

The next day, Ubar placed his mind into a relaxed state as usual. He killed flies and swooshed them away without conscious thought. He found he could listen to the petitioners while his eyes and hands tended to the king's tiny enemies.

After the people spoke, the king asked a few pointed questions, and Ubar listened. When the king ruled, Ubar was amazed at his wisdom. He seemed to always bring about a fair resolution. Ubar listened to the court all afternoon.

That evening, Yahatti called for Ubar.

"What did you learn today?" he asked.

"First, I learned that I can do my job while listening to the king's wisdom," Ubar said. "I think I have trained my muscles to react in unison with the flies and I am now able to learn even more. When I feel like my mind is full, the next day there is room for more. Therefore, I can let my instincts work while I learn to listen to the citizens and the king."

"Excellent," Yahatti said. "And what nuggets of wisdom did you gather today?"

Ubar recounted the details of one of the cases he had heard, listing the arguments made by the petitioners, the questions asked by the king, and finally the king's judgment.

"And what about the judgment," Yahatti asked. "Was it one you would have made?"

"No," Ubar said hesitantly. "I mean, after hearing the petitioners, I would sometimes feel that one of them was in the right. But after hearing the king decide in favor of the others, I would have to think for a long time."

"And what did you conclude?" Yahatti asked.

"I concluded that I have much to learn," Ubar said.

"Indeed," Yahatti said. "Now I wish for you to continue this part of your training. Listen to the king each day, and we will talk in the evenings."

Day by day, Ubar became better able to pay attention to the court proceedings while invisibly protecting the king from flies. And each night, Yahatti and Ubar discussed the cases, helping Ubar to understand the king's wisdom.

As the months went on, the former flymasters Rihat and Kuri encouraged Ubar to follow in their footsteps. It was as if they could sense Ubar's rising intelligence and his nightly meetings with Yahatti. They increased the pressure they were putting on Ubar to conform.

"Always mind your own business," Rihat warned. "Don't get big ideas. That's the way to survive forty years in the king's palace."

PRINCIPLE #2

THE OPPORTUNITY FOR GROWTH IS ALWAYS YOUR GREATEST BENEFIT.

I was never entirely sure I wanted to be a lawyer. Like lots of people, I entered my career with mixed motives. For one, I wanted a good education. I'd owned two small businesses before going to law school, and both were challenging. I wanted any learning that would give me a better shot at success. I also knew having a law degree was a ticket to steady employment.

So I worked hard, got good grades, clerked, and wrote a journal article, all in hopes of preparing myself for a successful life. Would I be a lawyer? Would I be an entrepreneur? I felt sure it would be the latter. I also felt sure a legal education would be a great start. We don't always know what we want to do when we grow up. I certainly didn't.

Even during law school, I kept scratching the entrepreneurial itch. I ventured into vacation rentals, which I would later leverage as a business owner. I learned to build websites, which resulted in meaningful income and other business ventures. But when I graduated from law school, I was still an entrepreneur raised by wolves. I was chasing dumb ideas, had little understanding of finance, and had many other gaps in expertise. Law school prepared me to be a lawyer, not an entrepreneur. Besides, I had about $100,000 in student loans with a monthly payment the size of a home mortgage.

So I did the sensible thing and found a job. I landed a position at a small law firm with very large clients and got down to the business of billing sixty hours a week. Welcome to the soul-crushing life of a young lawyer.

My advantage was that I was following the Way of the Flyswatter. I could see that lawyering—about as glamorous in real life as swatting flies—was only half my job. My real task was to learn everything I could about the business of a law firm. If I had any hope of forming an exit plan to entrepreneurship or working for myself as a lawyer, I'd need to milk my current position for all the experience, skill, and expertise it could offer. So, like Ubar, I became an "ethical thief." I made it my job to "steal" skills and knowledge that would become part of my career toolkit and eventually empower me to own my time, rather than grinding out hours for a paycheck.

Of course this is not stealing at all. Gaining knowledge and experience is a free perk that comes with every job. We're not talking about taking the company's intellectual property, such as client lists or proprietary processes. The point is to tap every resource available for insight, skill building, industry knowledge, and professional growth. When you leave your current employer, you'll turn in your laptop and all the data it contains. But whatever is in your head is yours to keep. Make the most of your opportunity to learn.

If you dream of moving from employee to owner (or even if you just want to climb the corporate ladder), your real job is to learn everything you can from your current situation. You are only required to do whatever is in your job description. But you are able to do more. That's right. Doing more than required for your employer is a privilege. It benefits you even more than it does your boss.

As you embark on this path, here are three imperatives to guide you.

Seek Opportunities for More

The first thing I learned as a newly-minted lawyer was that

many of my colleagues would always be flyswatters. There are a number of lawyers who will always need a job at a law firm. They like the work: drafting briefs, doing research, writing letters, or showing up for hearings. But they don't like people. They don't want to talk to clients. All they want to do is perform tasks in exchange for a salary. That's the essence of a job, after all. Do the work, get paid. It is high-paid flyswatting—at least it can be if that's how you approach it.

I wanted more, and I knew it. I was there to extract all the learning and skill I could while still performing my work at a high level. That meant, at a minimum, I had to master the art of swatting flies—that is, to become the very best lawyer I could be. That knowledge could come only from the best lawyers in the firm, who, ironically, often had no ambition to be self-employed. I needed to learn from the best flyswatters in the business.

I also needed to learn all I could from clients, who are the lifeblood of any business. I had to become an expert at client development and client relations. I also had to learn how to operate a law firm. Without that knowledge, I could only ever be a fly-swatting lawyer, never a business owner.

During my four years at that law firm, I went from the wet-behind-the-ears newbie to the lawyer with the most new clients every month. I learned all I could about every aspect of the legal business. I spent time with several mentors who had been successful lawyers, but who had also become entrepreneurs. After practicing law for a season, one of my mentors invested in a business, eventually becoming a nightclub owner and real estate developer. He made millions more as an investor than any lawyer grinding out billable hours every week.

I learned the most from my clients, and even went into business with one. That venture sold, and provided the financial means for me to leave the law firm and buy a property management business.

All of this can seem a bit intimidating at first. Like Ubar, you may wonder if it's possible or ethical to use your current job as a platform for preparing to move on. I'll say more about the ethics of this in a moment. As to whether you have the ability to do this—you do. Concentrate on your own work first. Like Ubar, you must first learn to swat files. That may take a while, possibly even years. You may hate your underlying work by the time you start to find ways to acquire the additional skills you need. The sooner you can add more skills, the quicker you'll have the opportunity to move up (at your job), over (to a lateral job with greater opportunities), or out (doing your own thing).

In time, you'll learn that your mind is an expandable compartment, just as Ubar did. The more you put in it, the more you'll find it can hold. The secret is to learn continually. Don't think of learning the way you may have thought about your formal education, a process to be completed before starting work. Learning is not about getting a certificate; learning is about getting real tools to empower you to have greater agency with your career and life. Your learning is open-ended. You'll be doing it for the rest of your life. The more you cram into that head of yours, the more room opens up for more.

As you look for opportunities to expand what you know at your current job, seek out mentors. Learn all you can from them. Some mentors will feed you without you having to ask. But most mentors will require you to come to them with an open mind and a closed mouth. You might be tempted to tell mentors what you know or think you know; a common mistake made by those hoping to impress their superiors. Mentors will avoid you if you do this. Come to them with true curiosity and an ambition to learn. Ask questions and listen carefully.

Keep Faith with Your Employer

As a subversive flyswatter, you live with an internal tension. Your true goal is to rise in your career. Yet you have an obligation to give your best in your current role. This is the tension Ubar was feeling when he asked Yahatti whether it was overstepping his place to learn about the king's judgments while serving as flyswatter. When you're hired to do one job, is it ethical to reach beyond it and use it as a platform for personal and professional growth?

Yes, provided you do so with integrity. Yahatti never suggested that Ubar should neglect his duties as flyswatter, only that it was possible to do even more than he was asked. As long as you continue to do your job well, it's perfectly fine to learn, grow, and accept responsibilities that go beyond it. In fact, doing this will make you a better employee.

In my case, it meant working along with the firm's culture and brand-building initiatives. We set goals and made plans for the future. I bought into all of that. Mentally, I knew I would not be around to make those plans reality. I was already working for myself, mentally. I had a different purpose for my own life. Yet I remained a team player and pulled my weight for the firm.

When you know your future lies outside the company, you immediately have a shelf life. That makes it challenging to keep swatting the flies and doing the day-in, day-out work you were hired to do. It's easy to mentally check out. Resist that urge. The moment you disengage from your current work, you take yourself off the path to a different future.

Look around your workplace and you'll probably see lots of stale and sour workers who have long outlasted their shelf life. In our parable, Ubar is already beginning to see this dynamic in Rihat and Kuri. Their goal isn't to move into a position of greater responsibility, nor even to do a good job swatting flies. Their goal is survival. If you mentally check out at work, that becomes your goal too. You'll be seeing how long you can hang in there before making your move to another situation. That attitude will actually undercut your aim.

It is up to you to manage your shelf life so you can keep on adding value and extracting skill.

Stay Focused on the Goal

The better you get at flyswatting, the more opportunities will come your way. You'll want to accept raises, bonuses, and promotions. As a diligent flyswatter, you are earning rewards. Take them and enjoy them. You should seek new opportunities at your current place of work. By doing so you'll learn even more, which is now your primary purpose for working. You'll be smarter. You'll look like the ideal employee. And as a result, you'll get promoted faster, paid more, and seen as the hot hand. Take advantage of this.

But here's the warning: Don't let the rewards of your current job distract from your goal of moving from wage earner to business owner. Your real goal is to have agency; the freedom to choose to work at your current job, work for yourself, or take another job that moves you upward.

I could tell you about many lawyers who found themselves trapped in the golden handcuffs of a six-figure job and a six-figure lifestyle. As the salary and perks gradually rose higher, they became like the proverbial boiling frog. Lulled to complacency by their lifestyle, they were distracted from the dream of entrepreneurship until it became too costly to make the leap.

You may find yourself at a crossroads where a tempting work opportunity diverges from your goal of entrepreneurship. Maybe it's a major promotion you never expected, or a partnership offer. Maybe it's moving to a new city to take over a division of the company. If you are the best flyswatter in the organization, listening and learning all the time, you will get noticed.

Should you accept the offer? Maybe. Just because work sucks doesn't mean you have to leave it immediately. That's the elegance of the flyswatter's path. It's good for employers when their employees have ambitions beyond their job. And that benefit may come back to the employee in raises, promotions, and opportunities.

If you take the next big opportunity, go big. But keep your ultimate goal in mind and don't let the golden handcuffs lock you into a place you never truly wanted to be.

Likewise, you may find yourself being recruited by another company. Great talent is in demand. You might find a lateral move that benefits you financially and gives you an opportunity to learn more. If you're so inclined, go for it. Again, be sure to keep your ultimate goal front and center. A subversive flyswatter is focused on learning everything they can so they have personal power; agency to move to any role. Most of us find our way out into the business world as owners, but plenty of people end up leading the companies they work for, or taking leadership positions at a new company.

Along this journey to self-empowerment, you'll encounter a variety of people. Some will become mentors and help you on your way. Others may offer enticements that tempt you to abandon your dream and help them to build theirs. You'll also find people who are not content with their situation and who have become complacent. Ubar has already begun to sense this in Rihat and Kuri. Both of these senior servants have stayed long beyond their shelf life.

People who think their only job is swatting flies will always be stuck swatting flies. When you have ambitions beyond your job, you will find these aggressively complacent coworkers intolerable. Worse, you may find them to be the single greatest obstacle to your own success.

Flyswatting in Action

Learning is the greatest benefit of employment. Look for opportunities to grow and improve yourself; these will pay dividends so much higher than a great health insurance package or the next incremental raise. You are always your greatest asset. Make sure you invest in yourself as much as possible, usually in the form of putting yourself in positions that will cause you to grow.

Some forms of thievery are okay. Ethical "stealing" means acquiring all the knowledge and skill possible from your job, then deploying these elsewhere when the time comes. This is not wrong; it is smart. Use your current circumstances to prepare for what's next—which ultimately should be a position of greater freedom.

Doing more than is required by your employer benefits you more than them. It gives you an advantage over your peers, makes you indispensable at your job, and affords you learning opportunities you otherwise would not get.

III

THE PLOT

For the next year, Ubar worked diligently swatting flies, listening and discussing the law with Yahatti. In the evenings, he socialized with friends on the palace staff. He had become acquainted with Anki, the chief cook, and several other senior servants. Ubar was well-liked, in part because of his relentless curiosity. He enjoyed watching other people exercise their skills.

One day while standing at his post, Ubar listened as the king presided over a dispute between two men over a business agreement. Having heard thousands of cases over the preceding months, Ubar discerned that one of the men was lying. He knew the king would see this also. But the king's questions seemed to indicate that he was preparing to rule in favor of the liar.

Ubar became distracted by his concern over the outcome of the case. He watched, as if in slow motion, as his horsetail whisk flicked the king's ear. It was the tiniest of touches, but Ubar knew at once it was a grave error.

The king paused mid-sentence. Citizens in the court looked up to see what had happened. Other servants and the guards froze. All eyes, including the king's, were focused on Ubar. He felt himself flush. His vision blurred to a tunnel. He bowed his head low in shame.

The king seemed to be taking in Ubar for the first time, as though he had been invisible for six years and had suddenly materialized from thin air. Ubar said nothing. He knew better than to blurt out an apology. He knew his position in the palace, perhaps even his life, hung in the balance.

At last, the king broke the silence.

"That has not happened for many years," he said thoughtfully. "It is a reminder that my unseen servants minister to me so that I am of clear mind to serve the people." The king looked around the court, smiling, then broke the tension with a laugh.

"You are good at your job," he said to Ubar. "So good that I have never noticed your presence."

Ubar dared to raise his eyes.

"And the timing of this disruption is a blessing from Anu. After this pause, I see this case in a different light," the king went on. With that, he turned to the two men and ruled decisively against the one Ubar believed to be lying.

As the two men left, the king whispered to Ubar, "Thank

you for being unseen. I am grateful for you."

At that moment, Ubar realized just how important his role was. He had always understood that his work allowed the king to be free from the small annoyance of buzzing insects. Now Ubar saw that there was more to it. His silent skill let the king have a clear mind. Without a competent flyswatter, the peace and justice that enabled Namir to prosper would be undermined. The king's flyswatter occupied one of the most important roles in the kingdom.

That night, there was a disruption in the servants' quarters. Rihat and Kuri both bemoaned the incident. Yahatti listened to their complaints.

"Many years have passed without the king feeling the brush of a hair," Rihat declared. "This is a serious breach. Some would call it an attack on the king."

Kuri nodded in dismay. "How is it possible?" he asked. "We have seen that his skills are impeccable. Was this done on purpose? Was he trying to get the king's attention?" They knew Ubar had high ambitions and this was a threat to both their sense of security and the pride they held in their stations.

"He must be removed from the court," Rihat declared. "Master Yahatti, you must find him a place in the kitchen. Or, better yet, in the stables."

"That's extreme," Yahatti said, trying to dismiss their concerns with a smile. But Rihat would have none of it.

"He must be removed!" Rihat insisted. "You are chief steward, Yahatti, but the boy works for us and we have decided he is to be released."

Yahatti knew full well that this demand had nothing to do with decorum or even the king's safety. Ubar represented an offense to the way of life these two men had embraced. They both feared and despised any servant who aspired to do more than his job. They believed in the pecking order of the palace staff, and they enforced it ruthlessly. Yahatti knew also that he could not fire Rihat and Kuri without the king's own blessing. Yet he would not let them dictate his decision as chief steward.

"I vouch for the boy," Yahatti said with authority. "He will remain the king's flyswatter."

The two men stood up and turned to leave. "You will regret this," Yahatti heard one of them mutter.

Later that evening, Yahatti spoke to Ubar privately.

"The incident is regrettable, my boy, but you are in no danger. I know it was done without malice."

Ubar nearly leapt from his chair.

"What?" he exclaimed. "Do you think I assaulted the king on purpose?"

"No, no," Yahatti said. "I think your instincts told you that the king was about to make a poor decision. So you allowed a single strand of the whisk to brush his ear, as if asking him to think further."

Ubar paused, considering this.

"How could I possibly know better than the king?" he asked. "I would never try to intervene with his judgment. He is wise beyond measure."

Yahatti nodded. "It was unconsciously done. You have

learned much from the king. Although you are just a flyswatter, you know his thinking. Your mind merely gave back to the king what he has imparted to you this past year."

Ubar was taken aback. He had never considered that being in the presence of a king would give him the mind of a king.

"Now you see my purpose in continuing your training," Yahatti said. "You are becoming a highly valued servant to the king, far more than a mere flyswatter."

Ubar could not find words.

"I must warn you though," Yahatti continued. "There are others here who do not like your growing intelligence—or your place beside the king."

"What does that mean?"

"It means you must be careful, and let your mind grow quietly. Be humble. Do not share your learning with those who will not understand it." Yahatti paused. "That could prove . . . quite dangerous."

"I do not understand," Ubar said. "All I want to do is serve the king. How could that anger anyone against me?"

"Small-minded people are very common. And they prefer one another's company. They are threatened by people of greater skill and intellect. They don't even know why."

And so, Ubar did as Yahatti said. He stood behind the king daily, expertly swatting flies and drinking in the king's wisdom. Week by week, he met with Yahatti to discuss his education. For several more years, he enjoyed the benefit of a secure position, a strong patron, and an unparalleled opportunity to learn from the king himself.

Over time, Yahatti became unwell. When the illness grew serious, he called for Ubar.

"My son, I have given you all the wisdom I can," Yahatti said. "I am confident you will continue well when I am gone."

"No, Master!" Ubar protested.

"Yes, it is so," Yahatti said calmly. "My days are coming to an end. I leave you with two parting gifts. Here is a small sum of money. Save it. Use it wisely when the time comes."

"Of course," Ubar said. "I am grateful."

"The other gift is a final word of wisdom. Hear me well," Yahatti said.

"I'm listening, Master," Ubar replied.

"You will do well in life, Ubar," Yahatti continued. "You have knowledge and skill. Yet remember this. The eagle flies highest, but always alone. There will come a day when you must spread your wings and soar without shame."

Three days later, Yahatti ascended to the heavens and entered the court of Anu.

After Yahatti's death, Rihat was elevated to chief steward based on his seniority. Within hours, the calm efficiency of Yahatti's management descended into a chaos of rumors, complaining, and gossip. Remembering Yahatti's parting words, Ubar kept his distance, going quietly about his work and keeping his own counsel.

A few days later, Rihat instructed Ubar to fetch tea for

the king before taking up his post as flyswatter. Ubar ran dutifully to the kitchen to get some tea from Anki.

The cook was puzzled by this. "This is not your place, Ubar. Dining stewards tend to the king's food and drink. Besides, he never takes tea at this time of day."

"I know that," Ubar said, "but I'm on orders from Rihat himself."

Anki shrugged and set to work. Ubar waited anxiously for the tea, knowing time was short. When Anki finished, Ubar snatched the tea service and raced to the king, hoping to make it in time.

From the doorway to the court, Ubar observed the king shooing a fly that buzzed around his head. Kuri, the former flymaster, stepped in with a whisk to swat it away.

Rihat appeared at Ubar's side.

"You are late!" he barked. "The king has been bothered by flies."

Ubar tried to speak, but Rihat continued his rant.

"What are you doing with that tea! You are not a kitchen steward. Are you trying to impress the king!"

"But you—"

"Silence!" Rihat commanded.

Ubar wanted to protest further, but the king was too far away to hear and had begun his audience with petitioners.

Rihat sneered at Ubar, "You worthless flyswatter. You do not deserve to be a servant of the great king. Be gone."

Ubar paced back to the kitchen, flushed with shame and anger. He returned the tea flask to Anki and told her what had happened.

"I knew something was wrong the moment you asked for tea," she said. Then in a lower voice, "I'm not surprised. Rihat has had it in for you for some time. You must go now, but be sure to stay in touch with me. There are many here who love and support you."

And so, Ubar packed his belongings and left the palace. He found his way to the home of his old master, Bashaa, and begged for a place of service.

"Of course," Bashaa said, delighted to see Ubar again. "I will gladly take the king's chief flyswatter into my home. You will supervise the flyswatters to my foremen. They will learn much from you."

Ubar did well in Bashaa's service and quickly realized that his skills made him nearly as valuable outside the palace as within. One evening over a cup of wine, he commiserated with Bashaa about his harsh treatment by Rihat and his cronies.

"It is always the way," Bashaa said. "These workers have no concept of freedom. All they can think of is guarding their place. It's all they have."

"What keeps them from learning more?" Ubar asked. "Why don't they seek to be their own masters?"

Bashaa shrugged. "It is a mindset, Ubar," he said. "But don't judge them too harshly. You were once on that path yourself."

PRINCIPLE #3

AMBITION ATTRACTS RESISTANCE.

The primary obstacle to your freedom will not be your boss or competition from other high achievers. It will be your own unwillingness to act. To quote Newton's first law of motion: "A body at rest will remain at rest, and a body in motion will remain in motion unless it is acted upon by an external force."[3] The inertia of complacency that characterizes so many workplaces will resist you—or anyone—who attempts to learn more, achieve more, grow more, or change more than those around you.

Be aware of your environment and how it is shaping you. To ignore this is to invite a slow decline toward settling for a life and career less than extraordinary. Complacent colleagues may work to undermine your efforts to better yourself as you make the shift from employee to entrepreneur. Often, this manifests in the petty shenanigans that are present in most workplaces: gossip, backbiting, and even bullying. Watch for these signs of toxicity, and if you find them, run. They are poison to the ambitious soul and will ultimately hold you back from what you deserve.

The Power of Inertia

When I was younger, I worked at a retail store at the mall while starting a landscape business on the side. A jealous coworker told our manager I had taken one of his sales as my own and improperly received the commission. This wasn't true. Appalled at the petty politics, I didn't yet understand how pervasive this sort of thing can be in any workplace.

You've probably seen the effect such politics can have on a high achiever who aspires to reach beyond what opportunities are currently available to them. The spirit of Rihat and Kuri are alive and well in many modern-day companies.

Years after my limited experience working in retail, I was lucky to find myself at a law firm and given the opportunity to rise within the company. Eventually, I was able to make a voluntary exit when I determined I'd gained all I could from that phase of my life. But such an exit didn't come without some resistance. If you follow the Way of the Flyswatter, you'll almost certainly face similar challenges and will need to be ready for the unexpected.

You must always be preparing yourself for what comes next. Learning new skills, gaining a wide variety of experiences, and networking with potential allies in your journey, all while taking on new responsibilities—these efforts position you for future success. Always be ready for change, and you'll have nothing to worry about when it comes.

During the time I was thinking of moving on from the law firm, I became aware that several other lawyers were also planning to leave. They intended to start another firm by taking a substantial number of clients with them. They offered me a role, which I declined politely. I'm not sure if they were fed up with the inertia they saw in leadership or were just eager to move from employee to owner. Either way, I wanted no role in such a schism.

I did, however, feel some obligation to explore how the senior partner was handling the issue. I knew that one of the lawyers involved in the plan had asked to become a partner in the firm. At a one-on-one meal with my boss, I hinted strongly that it might be wise to grant the partnership. "After all," I said, "he could take a bunch of clients and leave." I didn't want to betray the confidence of my colleagues. Their plan was not illegal in any way. But I wanted to see if my boss would accommodate new partners or risk losing clients.

He insisted that no clients would leave the firm. Instead, he disparaged the lawyer who wanted to be partner. I realized I was having dinner with Rihat, and decided to keep quiet the rest of the evening. I knew that I might someday be the subject of discussion. I had no better chance of becoming a partner than the lawyer who had been bold enough to ask for it. To stay with that firm would have been as pointless as Ubar continuing to work for Rihat. No matter how well I did, I would not rise in the business, be paid my full worth, or be respected as a partner in the firm. There was too much resistance in my path. It was time to get out.

Aspiring flyswatters and complacent coworkers (or bosses) simply don't mix. Inertia in the workplace is toxic for anyone with an ounce of ambition. When you can sense inertia taking over, you'll need to work on a plan to move on sooner rather than later. As an employee, you should have an exit plan that you are developing even while you are happily doing your job swatting flies, learning and growing. Remember, you don't want to wait until you can't gather the energy to open the front door to your office.

You Need an Exit Plan

I like the term "exit plan" for a lot of different reasons. It's a phrase that says, "I have a plan" and, "I have agency" at the same time. Business people know what an exit plan is. For an entrepreneur, the exit plan involves planning to build or grow a business to a point where it is sustainable using other people's labor.

That's the difference between employment and ownership. It's also what gives the business value so it can be sold. A business will generate income while you grow it and create a handsome payday when it's time to make another exit. But employees rarely think in terms of an exit plan, other than how to get promoted or who they need to impress to get a raise.

You need an exit plan. And it's as easy to do as following Ubar's path, even though Ubar didn't know that his mentor was putting him through a journey that he couldn't see. You'll choose to take this path as part of your intentional exit plan.

A New Mindset

The first step in your exit plan is to change your mindset from that of an employee to that of an owner. Employees don't think about themselves as operating a business, or even as taking part in operating one. They think of going to work as a job, an exchange of labor for money. If they have ambition at all, it's the ambition of Rihat. Keep doing what you're doing, work the system, climb the ladder, get one small raise after another, get a promotion here or there, and one day you can retire. That's the exit plan of most employees.

You need a better plan than that if you hope to have agency, control your time, and have the life you want.

Skill Acquisition

Ubar did some smart things while serving as a flyswatter. Think about the steps that prepared him for a soft landing when Rihat booted him from the palace door. He had become an expert flyswatter, so he had a marketable skill. He drank in all the learning he could, and not just from the king. He learned from Yahatti and Anki. He even learned from his frenemies, Rihat and Kuri. Learn all you can. Master your job and your boss's job. This is a big step in your exit plan.

Mentors

Ubar also found mentors in Yahatti and Anki. He sought their advice. He took direction from them, even though he didn't report to them. And he learned to steer clear of Rihat, Kuri, and their ilk.

All the players in your work life are critical to your exit plan. They can help or hinder your progress. Engage with smart, ambitious, positive, ethical people. Make them your friends and mentors. Learn all you can from them. While doing this, identify and avoid complacent workers. Their dour negativity is contagious; you don't want it to infect your thinking. And the closer you are to them, the more jealous and resistant they are likely to be.

Thanks to his relationship with Yahatti, Ubar was able to gather at least a few resources. Yahatti's gift of money gave him some options when the time came to leave. You'll need resources too, so look for ways to store them up.

I was able to do that by entering into a business opportunity with a client. He had a run-down plant nursery that needed some attention. I took over the business, revitalized it, and sold it within six months for six figures, all while keeping my day job at the law firm. I used the money from selling the nursery to buy a property management business.

So when it came time for me to leave the law firm, I had a financial base to start from. I knew I would only need a couple of clients to begin a solo law practice. I could even use the same office as the property management business and work side by side with my wife, which paved the way for my eventual exit. As the saying goes, you have to make hay while the sun is shining, using the resources at your disposal as they present themselves.

In other words, you'll need something to start with. I could not have started a law practice of my own if I had been a typical drone-type employee. I was awake to the opportunities around me. I was attune to the things I could gather from my experience. I learned the business of the firm. I learned how to land clients. I learned everything I could before I left, and then had it all in my tool chest for when I was working for myself.

Networking

Ubar began to do informally what he would later learn to do with intention—building a network. By making friends with Anki, he gained a valuable ally. When I was at the law firm,

I was the guy getting the new clients. I learned how to be a good lawyer by working directly with a client base I could call my own. I never planned to take them with me, but I did want to leave with a network of good relationships. Sooner or later, we all need the strength of a network to achieve our goals. Build yours now.

The Miserable Bargain

Most employees and employers are in a stalemate of sorts. The employee gives just enough effort to keep their job, and the employer pays just enough to keep them around. This arrangement stifles growth and creativity, and it will sooner or later breed the kind of toxic behavior that drives high achievers out the door.

When you find yourself in such a situation, realize that you are enabling the problem and must begin to move in another direction if you want something different. You don't have to jump ship right now, but begin formulating your plan so that you'll be ready to execute when the time comes. Because, as Ubar discovered, what comes next may surprise you.

Flyswatting in Action

Ambition attracts resistance. Flyswatters always face challenges, the greatest coming in the form of inertia. Be aware of what's holding you back, and be sure not to tether yourself to any relationships or circumstances that will slow you down.

Prepare for your exit sooner rather than later. You never know when the unexpected will come. And you always need to be ready.

Think like an owner, not like an employee. Give up the miserable bargain, and begin investing in a brighter future for yourself—now.

IV

THE CRAFTSMAN

As Ubar supervised the work of Bashaa's flyswatting crew, he had time to observe how other flyswatters used the whisk. For years, Ubar had refined his own technique. Yet most flyswatters, he realized, could not match his level of skill. They used the whisk to shoo flies, but most lacked the deftness to use it as a whip, striking individual flies in midair.

Ubar recalled a case he had heard once while attending to the king. It involved two men who each claimed to have invented a more efficient plow that could be pulled by just one ox or donkey rather than a team of animals. That day was an epiphany for Ubar. He had never thought of how someone might change a tool to make it better. The idea of creative innovation stuck in his head. Now he had a chance to apply it.

Ubar took some worn-out whisks and began to experiment with them. On some, he wove together several strands of horsehair to make a longer, thinner strand. It now resembled a miniature version of a drover's whip. Ubar found it much easier to strike individual flies.

On other whisks, he added more strands and shortened their length a bit, making it a bushier tool. With this, he could make broader strokes than with a conventional whisk, shooing flies much as a horse does with its tail.

After some experimentation, Ubar showed his designs to Bashaa.

"The ideal is to have two whisks," Ubar explained. "I use this one in my left hand. With its short handle and bushy tail, I make frequent broad strokes to keep most flies away from the foreman."

Bashaa played with the whips and listened, nodding.

"This one I use in my right hand," Ubar continued. "With its long, thin whip, I can make accurate shots close to the forman's body. It strikes the flies like an arrow."

Bashaa admired Ubar's handiwork.

"You have done well. Before we risk putting this in your flyswatters' hands, use it yourself on my lead foreman. He will put up with a few mistakes with the hope that your invention helps his flyswatter do a better job."

Ubar was delighted at the idea, and agreed.

For the next few weeks, Ubar left the work of supervising

flyswatters to an assistant and took up his place behind the lead foreman, once again swatting flies. In time, Ubar trained two of his best flyswatters to use the new whisks. They were delighted with how simple they were, and their foremen were pleased with the results.

Upon hearing the positive reports, Bashaa approached Ubar with an idea.

"I want to take your new whisks to the marketplace," Bashaa said. "One of my cousins is a whisk maker. He can produce the whisks for us, and only for us. I have a vendor who can sell them in the marketplace. I'll pay you a fee for each whisk I can sell. That way, we both can profit from the venture. If you also invest some of your inheritance from Yahatti, you'll make more as my partner."

Ubar was pleased with the arrangement. He knew that Bashaa would make more money on the whisks than he would, but Bashaa was also taking the risk and doing the work. Ubar didn't need to do anything more, yet he would receive payments. So Ubar went back to work supervising and training flyswatting employees, slowly integrating his new invention throughout Bashaa's business.

Meanwhile Bashaa, skilled as he was at business arrangements, saw to it that the new whisks were offered in every marketplace in the city. When it became known that the new whisks had been invented by the king's own flyswatter, and people saw how effectively they worked, demand for the invention spread like wildfire.

After less than a year, Bashaa invited Ubar to a formal

dinner. "You have made me quite a sum of gold, my boy."

Ubar was pleased with himself. He recalled Rihat and Kuri's jealousy and how they would not have been pleased with his invention, even though it would work better for protecting the king from flies.

"I'm not sure you understand much about money though," Bashaa said. "You are not a merchant. But the time has come for you to become a businessman." Bashaa took a heavy satchel from his side and put it on the table. It chinked when he set it down.

"This is your gold, my boy."

Ubar was shocked.

"All this?" he asked. "How much is it?"

"It is enough to buy this house." Bashaa paused for effect, then continued, "Plus some horses, a cart, and the cook's wages for a year." Bashaa watched Ubar's expression turn to wonder. "And even more than that, my boy."

Slowly, it dawned on Ubar that he was no longer a servant. He was a business partner to Bashaa, and a citizen of means in his own right. He was not sure how to process everything all at once.

"You have made me rich as well," said Bashaa. "I had money before, but much of what I made was put back into the business to keep everyone employed and to do my part for the city. Now I have the means to do even more. I have struck a deal to sell our whisks in our neighboring kingdoms. We may not make as much from each sale, but we will sell many, many more whisks."

Over the next few years, Ubar and Bashaa both prospered from the arrangement. Ever the learner, Ubar gained wisdom as well, learning the secrets of trading from Bashaa. As Ubar's wealth grew, his stature in the city also grew.

Yet Ubar remained cautious with his money, perhaps mindful of how quickly his place at the palace had been taken from him. Bashaa thought him a bit too wary.

"You are young and should invest, Ubar," he said. "Think of what you could do with more gold."

"But I'm comfortable now, Uncle," Ubar replied. "Why take chances?"

"You sound like those old servants at the palace," Bashaa teased. "Be careful that your caution does not make you complacent, Ubar. Your comfortable life will grow smaller and smaller if you do not venture out from time to time."

PRINCIPLE #4

CAPITAL COMES IN TWO FORMS: COMPETENCE AND CONNECTION.

Many employees dream of becoming employers, but most never do. The reason is simple. They're convinced they need a "big break" in order to venture out with an idea or product. They're waiting to wake up with a stroke of genius, a killer concept that will become the next hot product. I call this lottery-ticket mentality the Shark Tank Myth.

Shark Tank, as you probably know, is a TV program that features would-be entrepreneurs pitching their big idea to a panel of venture capitalists. The contestants hope their idea will receive financial backing. All they need, they're thinking, is one good push from investors. When they launch their miracle product, they'll be set for life.

I worked with a guy named Adam who talked about getting on *Shark Tank* almost daily.

"What's your idea?" I would ask.

"I don't know yet," he'd say. "But when I have the idea, I'll get on *Shark Tank* and get it launched. I'm certain of it!"

Adam didn't seem to realize that when the sharks invest, they don't just hand money to the entrepreneur. They put money into the business, buying a substantial share of the ownership. With that investment comes the expectation that the entrepreneur will do the heavy lifting.

The entrepreneur does the work, takes a paycheck, and makes the business a success. If it fails, the entrepreneur gets nothing. If it succeeds, the entrepreneur gets only the share of profit they have left after the investors get paid. Getting investors to put money into your business idea is not a get-rich-quick arrangement, and it's not a guarantee of success. Investors don't prove the worth of your idea. The market does.

The Shark Tank Myth is a major distraction from building a real exit plan that enables employees to eventually leave their jobs and become fully independent. You shouldn't spin your wheels trying to come up with the next big thing. That's a waste of time and energy. In fact, the ticket to your next success is likely right under your nose, even if it's at a job you don't like.

Leveraging the Mundane

Ubar's invention was not a new product or a revolutionary idea. It was the refinement of a device that had been around for ages. It was the culmination of his years of experience as an expert flyswatter. And when Ubar created it, his initial vision was rather limited. All he wanted was to improve the work of the flyswatters under his supervision. Ubar leveraged something he learned from his mundane job to create something of value.

What was Ubar doing in those early days with Bashaa? He was leveraging the expertise he had taken with him from *years* of work as the king's flyswatter, which allowed him to create a product that offered real value to the marketplace—other flyswatters like himself. Then he partnered with Bashaa in marketing the product, allowing Bashaa to do the work while he was paid a royalty.

That's an entirely different arrangement than what we see on a typical episode of *Shark Tank*.

Ubar didn't go into the business of marketing products, something he knew nothing about. He leveraged the capital he had: his expertise as a flyswatter. And rather than taking his product blindly to the marketplace, he leveraged another key source of capital: his relationship with Bashaa.

Competence and connection are the lifeblood of

entrepreneurship. Most would-be business owners focus only on financial capital, believing any product will be successful with enough money behind it. That's just not true.

Here's a real story of one of my business partners who gathered competence and relationships at his job before launching his own business.

Nate, my business partner and longtime friend, was still in college when he got a job doing internet marketing. He threw himself into it and learned everything he could. He followed the path of the flyswatter to a T, attending industry events, masterminds, and meetups, learning all he could from the more experienced people around him. Along the way, he made a lot of contacts in the business and even a few friends.

As Nate's expertise grew, he became highly competent in his field within a few short years. He also had gathered a vast network of associates in the industry because of his willingness to both learn and share information. When the company he worked for was sold, the founders asked him to join their next venture as a co-owner. And there it was: he leveraged his current position to move into the next thing. Flyswatting 101.

In the new position, Nate was able to take his flyswatting to the next level. He learned even more as a co-owner than he had as an employee, and his network expanded exponentially. By the time he exited that company, Nate had all the resources he needed to start a business of his own. He had financial capital from his earnings, a high level of competence in internet marketing, and a network that included the biggest players in that space.

Nate was able to create his own agency, doing exactly what he had done for others first as an employee and then as a partner. Within a few months, Nate had a string of clients, several employees, and an office buzzing with life. Since then, Nate has started, grown, and sold three additional agencies, all using the tools he obtained from his first "boring" job in that industry.

If you ask most successful entrepreneurs about their origin story, they'll tell you something similar to Nate's story. It starts by leveraging the capital you have at your disposal, and then expanding your relationships to build a network that extends beyond the borders of your job.

The Smallness of "Big" Ideas

The "big thing" you will eventually do as a business is not getting on *Shark Tank.* It's almost certainly not a radical idea, paradigm-shifting concept, or revolutionary product. Your big thing is probably right under your nose. It is likely tied to what you already do, who you already know, and a network of relationships you already have. If you don't have skill and goodwill with others, *Shark Tank* won't help you. And if you don't have competence and relationship capital right now, money capital won't do you much good. You'll need to work at your job before you can take an exit to self-employment.

Your job, in addition to doing the work you're being paid for, is to develop those things now. Competence and relationships are the capital that will build your future business. These are the keys to having agency: the freedom to choose to stay at a job, go to a new job, or go out on your own.

Flyswatting in Action

Entrepreneurs need two forms of capital: competence and connection. You have to get good at something, then find people who can help guide you in your journey. Don't prioritize skill acquisition at the cost of forming vital relationships (or vice versa). And don't assume that money covers every problem. Financial capital will follow the skills you hone and relationships you build.

Don't neglect the mundane. Leverage the ideas and people that are close at hand. That's all you usually have to work with—and it's enough to begin.

Your "big idea" is probably something very familiar to you, not a crazy idea or stroke of genius. Don't ignore the obvious.

V

THE MYTH OF INTENTION

"Be careful that your caution does not make you complacent, Ubar. Your comfortable life will grow smaller and smaller if you do not venture out from time to time."

When Bashaa uttered those words, Ubar became defensive.

"I'm not complacent, Uncle!" he insisted. "I have plans, many of them."

"Really?" Bashaa asked. "Let me hear them."

"Not now," Ubar said, becoming a little annoyed. "I'm working on ideas. I'll let you know when the time is right."

With that the conversation ended, but Bashaa's words

echoed in Ubar's mind for weeks. For years, Rihat and Kuri had told Ubar that job security was an employee's paramount concern. Stay where you are. Do what you're told. Mind your own business. And someday you'll get a promotion. Continue that plan for life, and you can probably retire with a small pension. What could be better?

Ubar had been mistrustful of Rihat and Kuri almost from the beginning, but their dour mindset had affected him more than he'd realized. Ubar always felt that his second assignment from Yahatti, learning the king's ways, was risky. After he'd been released, he was sure of it. He should have kept his mind closed and his mouth shut. If he had, he would never have struck the king's ear, never been entrapped by Rihat's scheme, never terminated from his secure job at the palace.

Now that Ubar had some financial means, his instinct was to preserve his wealth. It was true that he had ideas from time to time. He had thought briefly of investing his money in a house. Bashaa had said there was more than enough to build a fine home, which could then be sold for a profit.

But Ubar knew little about building, and less about selling houses. He wondered if it would be possible to create a more refined whip for cattle drivers, similar to his flyswatter design. Yet he didn't know anything about the leather trade or the cattle business.

Deep down, Ubar was still conditioned to play it safe. His palms got sweaty when he thought of taking risks. Where had that landed him?

Bashaa continued to coach Ubar, giving him examples of the business deals he was working on throughout the city. Bashaa's stories were varied and sometimes extremely colorful. In one deal with a spice importer, Bashaa had doubled his money in a single trade. At the same time, he'd lost his entire investment on a purchase from an itinerant shepherd.

"The goats looked perfect," Bashaa said, "the best I'd seen. But it turned out they'd all eaten a toxic plant while being driven into town. They were dead by sundown." Bashaa laughed aloud at the memory. "The poor shepherd had no idea. The weed looked just like a carrot stalk. We bought them fair and square. You win some and you lose some.

"The truth is," he continued, "most ventures were somewhere between those extremes. I learn a little every time, win or lose. And look at me. I'm doing well!"

The idea of buying a herd of livestock and having them all die gave Ubar a knot in his stomach. But when Bashaa told of some investments that returned his money ten times over, Ubar began to understand the game better. Ubar even began to connect these stories to the disputes he had heard in the king's court. When deals went bad, the people involved needed wisdom from the king on how to allocate responsibility.

As time passed, Bashaa's wisdom began to outweigh the ghost voices of Rihat and Kuri. Perhaps Bashaa was right. If Ubar remained hesitant, thinking only of the worst outcome and jealously guarding his gains, he might well end up with nothing. There really was no safety in complacency. He needed to venture out somehow.

One morning Ubar approached Bashaa before commencing work.

"Uncle, I would like to start another business venture with you."

"Excellent, my boy. We will start today."

"Today?" Ubar asked, a little unsettled.

"Don't worry," Bashaa laughed. "You won't have to spend your money today. I am meeting with a caravaner this morning. He has wares from far away to show me. Together we can decide what our next investment will be."

PRINCIPLE #5

INTENTION IS NOT ACTION.

The Myth of Intention is another trap for would-be entrepreneurs. This is the belief that daydreams are the same as plans, that wanting to create an exit plan is the same thing as doing it.

There are probably many sources for the origins of this modern myth. Napoleon Hill's approach in *Think and Grow Rich* involved a mystical element of connecting thoughts like a mental antenna to a universal intelligence. Rhonda Byrne's *The Secret* espoused the law of attraction, where we manifest what we intend. A popular evangelical Christian sect called

Word of Faith embraces the belief that God gives us whatever we ask for. It is also a theme of many new-age mantras that we can achieve what we want if we set our intentions and allow the thing we want to manifest itself in our lives. We tend to like this message because it doesn't require learning, planning, or execution.

Many people succumb to this for a variety of reasons. For one, we get a psychological boost from making a decision. Feeling stuck, whether that's in a job, a relationship, debt, or any other circumstance, feels paralyzing. The moment we decide to break free from that circumstance, we feel better. We feel empowered. We actually envision ourselves in our future state: owning a business, perhaps no longer in a toxic relationship, or debt-free. That feels good. That's why so many people begin diets on a Monday or swear off alcohol on Sunday morning. Sadly, people mistake that temporary psychological relief for a real action.

This is not to say that intention doesn't matter. It most certainly does. Intention is a key starting point for being empowered to act. You have to get your head around something and fully embrace it before you can do the work of accomplishing anything.

The thing people miss is that many modern ideas around intention treat it like a magical genie or a spiritual incantation. For example, some people miss Napoleon Hill's point about learning, growth, and persistence. He actually doesn't say that when you have a thought it automatically becomes reality. Hill's philosophy requires acquiring skill and personal growth, and sticking with your intention in the long haul. His book is actually full of job advice, and it predicts portable skills his readers will need to flourish.

Certainly, there are a few people who find unsought opportunities that produce results with little effort. The fantastic tales that accompany these philosophies of intention are inspiring. And who knows? Some of them may actually be true. But that's simply not how opportunity works for the majority of people. You can't wait for something to happen, hoping your intention is heard by the universe. The universe expects you to act.

By and large, intention only has value when it's followed by action. Goals are not achieved by writing them down; they're achieved by taking practical steps toward their fulfillment. Your exit plan doesn't come to pass when you decide you will do something. It happens when you actively execute that plan. For every self-employed person who got there seemingly by accident or luck, there are a million others who did it by executing on a clear plan. And there are tens of millions more who got nowhere by waiting around.

I had a conversation many years ago with a colleague who was entering the real estate business. It was during the financial crisis that began 2008 and continued for several years. I had spent the years prior to that investing in real estate, and I understood the business quite well. In our conversation I asked my friend questions about marketing, her plan for lead generation, how she would deal with the constraints of a down market, and tough lending conditions.

Her response was that she was not going to focus on those negative things. She was going to "manifest success." She had set her intention, she believed that she would attract the right people, and that the deals would flow. This is one of dozens of similar conversations I've had over the years. I can't tell you whether any of these manifestors actually achieved their goals, but I can tell you that this is not a reliable method for achieving yours.

Again, this is not to say there is no value in having a strong intention. Your will really is the starting place for your move from an employee—subject to someone else's whims—to an empowered leader in a career where you have agency. In my opinion, the only thing worse than the Myth of Intention is having no intention at all. Most people who are working away at their job have no fully-formed intention about what comes next, personally or professionally.

If that describes you, you aren't alone. Corporate America doesn't want you to set intentions on anything other than getting a good annual review and a small pay increase. The education system wants you to focus on getting good grades, instead of accomplishing something with what you are learning.

Marketers want you to desire their products and services. We have been bred like cattle to become human resources for the advancement of others. The system is built to keep your energy channeled at producing more, then deploying your hard-won resources back into the system.

Even your retirement plan is probably not intentional on your part. Your money goes to a 401(k) that funds the companies that sell you things you don't need. That leaves you lacking the financial freedom to do what you might actually want to do with your life.

Like a boat without a rudder, most people are tossed along rather than piloting their own course. Even the New Age manifest-your-intention folks are more likely to succeed than those with no intentions at all. Maybe that's why it so often seems that their way is working. But the real power in intention is when it becomes a starting point for action. Without action, which necessarily involves some risk, no change is possible.

Ubar had no intention when he was a flyswatter. He was lucky to have a mentor who saw a greater path and convinced him to move on. He resisted, almost taking the safe, mindless path of Rihat and Kuri. But he followed Yahatti's plan.

After he was ejected from the king's palace, he relied on Bashaa's plan. He had not yet realized that he needed to take control of his future and make plans to achieve his goals. It took real courage for him to break out of his comfort zone and achieve something more by moving beyond what he had already gained. Ubar was willing, finally, to tie his goals to action. I'll bet you are too.

What will become of Ubar's next big venture? Will his risk pay off, or will he lose his capital on poisoned goats?

Let's find out.

Flyswatting in Action

Intention is not action. All the best ideas in the world don't amount to anything without a willingness to take the first step.

It is not possible to "manifest" success by thought or desire alone. You have to work toward what you want, one small step at a time.

Successful entrepreneurs turn their dreams into goals, then make plans they can achieve, and execute those plans.

VI

THE WISDOM OF THE FOREST

Ubar accompanied Bashaa to his meeting with the caravanner. The man wore a colorful tunic and spoke with a thick Egyptian accent. Over tea, he regaled them both with stories of his adventures on the caravan route. Afterward, the man showed Ubar and Bashaa his product, a thin rope made from fibers that grew along the River Nile. It was lightweight and durable. The merchant promised a steady supply if Ubar and Bashaa would agree to become his partners in Namir.

Bashaa and Ubar discussed the opportunity as they ate that evening.

"This is a great prospect," Ubar said, barely concealing

his excitement. "The price is excellent. I think we could corner the market with this lighter rope."

"Not so fast, Ubar," Bashaa said. "I realize this does not sound risky, but you and I are not experts in the rope business. The uncertainty here is not what we know, but what we don't know."

Ubar replied, "But is that not always the case?"

"No," said Bashaa. "We invest in what we know so that we diminish risk. When we do not know the market, we seek advice from those who do."

"How do we do that, Uncle?"

"We pay a wise advisor who has worked in that business—one we believe is neutral about the product, the market, and the individuals involved."

Ubar leaned back to ponder this advice from his mentor.

"Is this a deal worth paying for advice?" Ubar asked.

"I believe it is worth the investment to seek counsel," said Bashaa. "This opportunity has great potential, but only if we enter it with a well-informed plan."

Several days later, the two called on a business associate of Bashaa, Miri, who had spent a number of years trading in rope. They showed him the rope and asked his advice.

"We can get a great supply of this rope very affordably," Bashaa said. "What we want to know from you is how this rope might do in the local market. Do you think the builders and tradesmen of Namir would buy it? It's much lighter than our ropes, and much less expensive."

The trader handled the rope, stretching it, pulling at the strands, running it through his hands.

"This fiber is not as strong as our native material," he said. "And see here? The strands come unwound too easily. The craftsmanship is inferior."

Bashaa and Ubar nodded. "So that's that," Ubar said disappointedly.

"Not necessarily," the trader said. "This rope would certainly not bear the weight of stones or timber, and it wouldn't restrain a team of oxen. But it could still be useful."

"And what about this caravanner from Egypt?" Bashaa asked. "Do you know him?"

"Yes," the trader said. "I have dealt with Ahmed before. He always delivers as promised. But you must not trust his price. He will overcharge you if he can."

Bashaa and Ubar questioned the man further, then paid his fee and retired to Bashaa's home.

"I think we should not do this deal," said Ubar. "If it's not useful to builders, we have no market."

"There is good reason not to," Bashaa replied. "However, let us explore whether there is a market for this cheaper rope. Perhaps other customers might find a use for it."

For several weeks Ubar and Bashaa showed samples of the rope to neighbors and friends, asking if they would like some. They found many people eager to try it. Some could not afford the higher quality ropes available in Namir. Others wanted it for smaller tasks, such as bundling cloth or securing small loads on a donkey. Household servants were especially interested.

Ubar even showed a sample to his old friend Anki, the king's cook.

"I can think of a thousand uses for this cord," she said excitedly. "I will buy this one from you right now!"

Having found that there was indeed a market for the lighter, lower quality material, Bashaa and Ubar set about forming a plan. First, they negotiated the import deal with Ahmed. As Miri had said, Ahmed was prone to inflating his price. Pointing out the inferior quality, plus the fact that they would have to carve out a market from scratch, Ubar and Bashaa were able to get much more favorable terms, with Ahmed agreeing to give the first delivery on consignment.

Then the two set to work finding partners. By leveraging Bashaa's network of merchants and Ubar's contacts at the palace, they secured additional financial backing and advance orders for two-thirds of their first delivery. Within a few months, their initial profits were distributed, and Ubar tallied up his return. He had more than doubled his investment, even after accounting for the payment to Bashaa's advisor and the sample ropes they had allocated to test the market.

It was not long before Ubar and Bashaa had spread their profits across a few other ventures. They were as smart as they could be about who they invested with and about the subject of each investment. They sought wise counsel on most deals, and spent their evenings talking about their various ventures.

Ubar was coming out of his safety mode of thinking. He realized how much of that safety was conditioned by fears instilled in him by servants like Rihat and Kuri. He realized these two men were not wise advisors, but scared servants who constantly imagined the worst. They built walls around their lives to insulate them from any potential loss or failure, and urged others to do the same as a way to affirm their own small-mindedness.

"We have done well, Uncle," he said over dinner one evening. "This could have gone much differently if we had not sought the advice of your friend Miri."

"It is the wisdom of the forest," Bashaa said. "Trees are strongest when they stand together. We strengthen ourselves when we draw advice and partnership from others."

"Indeed," Ubar said. "You have taught me to plan carefully and make use of many advisors."

Over the next two years, Ubar made far more than he lost and gained a great deal of confidence. He also earned a reputation as one of the most successful business people in the city.

PRINCIPLE #6

MAKE YOUR PLAN BEFORE YOU MAKE YOUR MOVE.

Remember my friend Cory, the software project manager who had enough of working for wages and playing it safe, so he quit? A few days after he walked away from his job, my friend asked me to lunch. He knew that I'd "gone rogue" and left my own secure job at the law firm to become an entrepreneur.

We sat down to eat in the seaside town of Encinitas, California. I had a surfboard in my car and planned to catch a few waves after we connected. But Cory had more than a how's-it-going conversation in mind. He was looking for the secret formula that would enable him to do what I'd done. I never did make it to the beach that afternoon.

Unfortunately, I didn't have a 1-2-3 plan to offer Cory. True, I had spent many years self-employed as an entrepreneur, and I was nurturing a small law practice that gave me the freedom to surf on a random Tuesday. But I had no secret formula to offer. I knew Cory needed to make his own plan, one that leveraged his unique capital in skill, knowledge, and relationships. He likely wouldn't succeed by taking the exact steps I took.

What I did have to offer were the principles I'd been gathering through my experiences as an entrepreneur, the principles I compiled in *The King's Flyswatter.* I knew that whatever he did next, Cory would have to leverage all the skills he had acquired as a project manager at a large software development company. To become a successful entrepreneur, he would need to make use of his relationships, his competence, and his finances. He needed a plan to put everything together into a compelling business idea. I told him that if he did this, he had the potential to build a business worth millions of dollars, all while living a life he had more control over.

Cory didn't know it at the time, but he was about to build a business that would set him down a path of independence and freedom for the rest of his life. Soon, with the right moves that he eventually made, he'd be more in control of his life and work than he had ever been. He was on his way to building a dream he could not even conceive of at the time. Along the way, he'd acquire other skills and relationships that would eventually afford him a place at the head of the table in his industry.

If you're thinking of walking away from your current job and *then* looking around for what comes next, be careful. You're far better off building a network and forming a practical plan while you still have a job. Yes, Cory pulled it off; but I could tell you of many would-be entrepreneurs who cashed out their retirement accounts to invest in real estate or start a business without a clear plan—and many failed because they didn't adequately assess the risks. They never shared their plan with anyone other than maybe a handful of friends who weren't really qualified to give advice on business ventures. Driven by the pain of a bad employment situation, they came up with something that made sense in their own mind, then took the leap.

This is dangerous, risky, and completely unnecessary.

Make your plan before you make your move, and vet that plan with competent advisors. This approach will mitigate your risk and exponentially improve your chances of success. Don't wait until your hand can't pull open the door to your office. Make a plan now, while you still have a job. The stakes are too high. Why roll the dice when you don't have to?

If Cory had read this book, he may have realized he could leave his job to become a consultant, using all of the skills and relationships he had developed at the job he hated so much. That's how most entrepreneurs go from employees to self-employed. Cory was a diligent saver, and smart with his money. So, he did know he could take some time to figure out what was next after he quit.

In addition to seeking my advice, Cory met with Steve, another entrepreneur. Steve asked him about what skills he had. It turned out that Steve needed someone just like Cory on a contract basis. So, Cory's first self-employed role was indeed using the skills he learned from his horrible job to work for himself as a consultant.

While being self-employed, and having agency and more free time, Cory was able to launch a business he had been studying. I joined him as founder in an audiobook business that would eventually sell for millions. And, since that time, we both continue to leverage our expertise in the audiobook industry. We are now both cofounders of other businesses that leverage the skills, network, and resources we gained from our previous ventures.

Seek Wise Counsel

Wise entrepreneurs know that they can't start "doing" until they have a plan in place that they can execute. They seek feedback and pay for advice whenever possible. They take their time, do their research, and pull the trigger when they've assessed the risks and rewards. Ubar was lucky to have his mentors lead him through plans they themselves had devised. But it was not until he fully engaged in the process of the rope venture that he clearly saw how to plan for success and mitigate risk.

If you're going to make a move, you need to acquire all the information you can, work your networks, and develop a strategy that has a good chance of success. Once Ubar learned how to succeed, he could repeat the process in other endeavors. This is a crucial evolution from an employee mindset to an entrepreneurial one. Most employees rarely participate in strategic planning for the organizations that employ them. Far too often, they are excluded from such processes regarding major decisions that affect the company's goals and strategic objectives. Usually, they are simply deployed on the plans already in place. Part of gaining autonomy, then, is understanding the goal setting and planning process behind whatever the organization is doing. Not only is this how businesses achieve success, but it's how individuals can manage risk.

A lot of people never do the things they dream about because they don't understand what it means to move from intention to action. You can have a big idea that leads to a very lofty goal, but this is not enough to achieve your dream. To get where you want to go, you need to make simple and executable plans that minimize risk and consider all potential outcomes. Then, each day you must follow the plan and measure the result. This is so painfully obvious and simple that most people just don't do it.

Ubar was fortunate to have good mentors who took him under their wings and advised him in his own plans. You may not be so lucky. If you don't have a mentor, don't sit back and wait for one to appear. Find yourself a Yahatti or a Bashaa, someone who has been down the road you hope to travel. Harvest the wisdom they have gained over years of doing what you hope to do. And don't merely show them your plan. Learn how they do it. Think of how Yahatti moved Ubar along in his career development, giving him one small assignment after another. Each small plan wove its way into a larger plan that continued to unfold in his life with each informed step he took.

Whether you are on a path to move through your job to become self-employed or you are someone who wants to rise in your career, you'll get there fastest and most successfully by following small but intentional steps that build momentum as you go. You are empowered, even if you feel that you are not. It is up to you to chart your course instead of waiting for mentors to do it for you. If you are lucky enough to have mentors who advise you, listen carefully and understand that they might be your Yahatti or your Bashaa. They may show you things you didn't know—or didn't know you didn't know.

Planning Diminishes Risk

All ventures involve risk, but planning diminishes it. There is no such thing as a sure thing. To move from employee to owner, you will need all the energy you get from having a clear vision. You'll also need a solid plan that will mitigate the risks and set you up for success. Take control of your work journey by making a plan even while you have a job; a plan that will enable you to take the leap to something better down the road, or even to self-employment. Before you make your exit, make an exit plan.

My friend Gabe masterfully planned his exit from investment baking, and it paid off handsomely. Gabe and I worked at the same company for several years. Gabe didn't like the way this company operated, which was typical for investment banks: focusing on how to dress, showing up at a stuffy office, following protocol that had no real meaning, and doing things he was told to do by people who had no idea why they did it that way in the first place.

So Gabe formulated an idea about what he wanted, an intention. He wanted to do meaningful work that was within his expertise. He wanted to work with solid, like-minded people. He wanted to control the use of his time and earn an income that correlated to the value he delivered.

Gabe wanted to go to the office only when necessary, not on a set schedule. And one more thing—Gabe wanted to bring his dog, Hank, to the office. I'd say Gabe had a robust set of intentions that ran counter to the expectations of nearly all investment banking firms. By traditional standards, Gabe was unemployable. If you walked into an investment bank and told them you wanted to make great money, show up when you want, wear what you want, and bring your dog with you, they'd laugh you out of their office. But Gabe set his mind on this goal.

Gabe didn't simply wish for that kind of workplace and wait for "the universe" to deliver. He made a plan. While still working at a job he didn't really like, Gabe spent several years digging deeply into every aspect of investment banking. He gained a thorough knowledge of the entire business, not just the requirements of his job. He followed the Way of the Flyswatter. Gabe was no clock-punching drone. He was an A-player in his company, which enabled him to develop a solid network of coworkers, clients, and industry leaders.

Considering Gabe's success in the company, his colleagues were surprised when he left his job at the bank. What was he going to do? Hang out his own shingle? Broker deals as a solo consultant? Nope.

Gabe had a different plan, one focused on acquiring what he intended. He started a service business doing a particular task that investment banks didn't do well: back office research and buyer outreach. This would be the type of business where no one cares what you wear or when you come to the office. Gabe and his partner built a small team and grew what is now a business that requires only a couple of days a week at the office—with his dog Hank. Gabe's income exceeds that of most investment bankers with traditional jobs. Someone recently asked him if his McLaren sports car has an Instagram page of its own. Obviously he is doing well, and he achieved that by taking what he learned at his job, using his network, planning his exit, and building a business that gave him the life he wanted to live.

Gabe had some very specific intentions. But he had something even more powerful. He had the discipline to put action behind those intentions. He learned, acquired skills, and eventually took the big step of leaving the investment bank and venturing out on his own.

From Employee to Entrepreneur

Let's say you have formed your intention to move from employee to owner. It's easy to get really excited about making a big move once you begin to envision that it's something you can achieve. You can't just take the big leap without a plan. But you can't sit around waiting for something big to happen. You must make it happen.

Successful entrepreneurs set a goal, then make a plan and, finally, execute the plan. It's incredibly tempting to act on emotion, quit on short notice, and launch a venture without an adequate skill-based understanding of the market you can leverage. You need all three. Skills. Network. Plan. Those are the three most powerful tools for success, whether you want to rise in your career or find a pathway to exit and work for yourself.

I am not telling you to put your dreams on hold. I am telling you that before you branch out, you need to acquire the primary capital you'll need to be successful: skill and relationships. Use your current job to develop both. Learn your job, your boss's job, and their boss's job. Get good at what you do. Make positive relationships with clients, customers, vendors, and colleagues. Finally, take all you have learned and make a clear, workable plan for launching yourself forward.

"Entrepreneur" does not mean "crazy risk taker." It actually means one who undertakes a project. You accept responsibility for something, assume some risk, and then think through how you're going to accomplish your goal. Successful entrepreneurs mitigate risk with a solid plan formed from the advice of knowledgeable people. To do anything else is to flirt with disaster.

Flyswatting in Action

Before you set out to accomplish the impossible, start with your skills. Get good before you start setting crazy goals.

Don't neglect your network. An important part of your capital is your connections, and this is especially true when considering those who can help you think through your plan. If you don't have a mentor or entrepreneurial advisor, find someone who has been where you want to go and share your plan with them before acting on it.

Dream, plan, execute: in that order. Big ideas are great, but remember that all giant leaps start with small steps.

VII

THE LIAR

One morning, Ubar and Bashaa met to review their current investments. Ubar was in high spirits because the most recent deals he had brokered with Bashaa were paying off nicely.

"Look, Uncle," he said. "I think we have developed the magic touch. We're coming out ahead every time."

"Now, lest we get too proud," Bashaa said, "I have some bad news. We have an investment that has gone to the dogs."

Ubar sat upright. "What?"

"Unfortunately, one of our larger investments has a problem," Bashaa continued. "The fellow we contracted with to sell cotton fabric is a bit of a fraud. It appears he has been living it up on our investment while the business languishes for lack of management. We must fire him and take over the business ourselves. Or we can decide to walk away and lick our wounds."

Ubar grew silent, his brow furrowed. He had had his share of losses when the market was poor. But he had never lost this much—and never in this way. He was upset that his money had been squandered by someone who acted so deceitfully. Worse, Ubar understood that he was responsible for this investment. The deal had sounded good, and the man came well recommended. Ubar had jumped at the chance to invest.

"I am angry, Uncle," he said to Bashaa. "I am angry at this man for defrauding us. And I am disgusted with myself for my lack of diligence."

"Don't take it too hard, Ubar," said Bashaa. "I am angry as well. But you will remember that these are risks we take in business, not unlike the poisoned goats. It is especially disheartening when the loss is not accidental, but the result of dealing with a fool. Now we must either absorb the loss or seek ways to recover it."

Over the next few days, Ubar ruminated on the situation and inquired further about the partner who sold them on the investment then wasted their money. It turned out that the man had a reputation as an excellent businessman. This bothered Ubar even more than the financial loss because it meant that the man could continue obtaining money from trusting business partners who were unaware of his fraud.

One evening Ubar said to Bashaa, "I think we should bring this man to justice."

"I'm not sure it's worth the effort," Bashaa replied. "We can afford to take a loss now and then."

"I know this is true, Uncle, but if we do nothing, this man will take advantage of others. We can put a stop to that."

Bashaa replied, "We do well not to spread rumors against a man of good reputation."

"I agree, which is why we should bring this case before the king. He will hear our cause and prove that this man does not deserve his reputation," said Ubar.

Bashaa sat back and stroked his chin, nodding in agreement.

The two spoke to others in the community and learned that the man would return to Namir in a month's time. When he arrived, Ubar and Bashaa gathered some associates and confronted him.

"What is this mob?" the man demanded. "I will not have this threat of violence!"

A nearby palace guard approached them. The man caught his attention and shouted, "I am being attacked by this group of unruly men!"

The guard looked around at the businessmen.

"You are in no danger, sir," he said. "These men are unarmed and are known to be businessmen of the city."

Ubar interjected, "Guard, we wish to bring a case before the king against this man. He defrauded us of our investment, spending it on his lavish lifestyle rather than investing in the trade of goods he promised."

"I have a sterling reputation as a successful businessman,"

the man protested. "I will not debase myself by listening to these accusations."

The guard knew that this was a common problem, one the king usually left to the marketplace to solve. Yet he remembered Ubar and decided to take action.

"I will escort you all to the court and let you present your case to the door guard. If the king wishes, he will hear you," said the guard.

The group walked to the palace and approached the portico outside the court where administrators and guards gathered to deal with city business.

The same exchange was made with the door guard and a palace administrator, who nodded as the parties made arguments. The two disappeared into the court, then returned a few moments later.

"The king will hear your case immediately," said the guard. "Follow me." He led the group into the court where the king was seated on his throne. Behind him stood a young flyswatter, working his dual whisk with patience and agility.

Ubar presented his case to the king, who did not appear to recognize him.

Then the accused man presented his defense. "I have been a well-known businessman in this city for many years. The investment made by Ubar and Bashaa was speculative and simply did not pay off. I warned them of this possibility and did all I could to protect their investment. There is no fraud here."

The king thought, then spoke, "I see other leading men

of the community present. Do any of you have evidence to present?"

A round-faced man stepped before the king and said, "My lord, I once invested with this man, and did not receive any return or any of my original investment. It was not a risky venture. I believe my money was mishandled."

The king replied, "Why do you say this only now and not when this occurred?"

"It was out of respect for this man's reputation. I did not want to speak ill of a man based on one bad experience."

The king waited, lost in thought. After some time, he spoke, "Any others?"

Another man rose to speak.

"I had the same experience, my king," he said. Then another man spoke, and another. Finally, the administrator who had heard Ubar's case at the portico spoke up.

"This is my story as well, my lord."

The king laughed and said, "Well, well. We have a businessman here who does not trade in goods, but in reputation. He has been selling himself to you all, and you have been too ashamed to do something about it."

"My lord," the accused man said, "I have been successful in many ventures and made much gold for my investors."

"We shall see," said the king. "I order an audit of this man's business to determine if he has simply been a bad investor or has misused the investments for himself. The court accountant will conduct an investigation. If the results are in his favor, we will restore this man's reputation. If it is not, his gold will be taken and given half to the investors and half to the poor, as is the law in this city."

As the group dispersed, the king took notice of Ubar.

"I know you," he said. "I recognize you now, my former flyswatter!"

Ubar was embarrassed and stepped forward with a low bow. "My king."

"I am glad to see you among the businessmen of the city and wish you well in this matter."

"Thank you, my king," said Ubar.

"I heard you have done well with your fly whisk invention. You have also grown into a man," said the king.

"Thank you, lord. I have invested in ventures with Yahatti's brother Bashaa, which brought us to your court with this unfortunate matter today."

"Ah, Bashaa, welcome!" said the king. "How I miss your brother. He was a great administrator. His death was a loss to all of Namir."

"Thank you, my king. He was your most loyal servant," Bashaa said, then paused. "We hesitated to bring this trivial matter to your court," he continued. "But Ubar wanted to put a stop to this man defrauding investors. We lost a little, but others could lose more if we kept silent."

"Wise of you both," the king replied. "That is why justice is so important to our kingdom. Go forth and all of you do honest business to continue to make this city the most prosperous in the land!"

Within a week's time, the court account's report vindicated Ubar and Bashaa, exposing the other businessman as a fraud. In executing his judgment, the king ordered that Ubar be in charge of distributing half of the man's gold to the poor.

Ubar used his time with the poor to tell them stories of the king's court. He found that the poor often followed the safe thinking of Rihat and Kuri, expecting that if they accepted their position in life and did what they were told, they would eventually gain a small increase in their wages. Ubar began teaching them to think differently.

"Do not believe that you have no choices in life," Ubar taught. "Look at me. I was once an orphan boy, virtually a slave in the house of Bashaa. Today he and I are business partners." Eyes widened in astonishment. These common people could not believe that Ubar had once been in their situation.

"Do not simply do your job, but always learn to do it better. And do not despise your work, however menial. Learn to do it well. This will be your stepping stone to a greater responsibility. And make friends with those who are doing well in life. Someday they will be in a position to aid you, or you them."

Thus Ubar's reputation continued to grow with the people, the businessmen, and the king. Each time the royal treasury had gold to disburse to the poor, the king's accountant entrusted it to Ubar. Within a few years, some of Ubar's students had become skilled in trades, others had been promoted to overseers, and some had become scholars. Some came to Ubar with business ideas, which he was happy to consider, and many of those investments prospered.

"Ubar," Bashaa observed one day. "You used to go into the city, searching for opportunities and investments. Now the city is coming to you!"

"It seems so," said Ubar, more puzzled than proud. "Yet I'm doing nothing more than I did as a servant in the palace. I am still learning every day."

PRINCIPLE #7

REPUTATION INVITES OPPORTUNITY.

As you move from employee to entrepreneur, half of your capital is in the relationships—the network—you form along the way. You need this relational capital as much, or more, than you need financial capital.

In practical terms, your network provides a host of benefits. You gain knowledge from your mentors. You get referrals from your contacts. You share insights with your peers. You will even find clients or customers among the people you know, or who know you. The larger and healthier your network of relationships, the more capital you have for launching your business.

That makes building a network one of the most valuable things a businessperson can do. Your network is more valuable than money. One successful entrepreneur went so far as to tell me that he didn't worry about the success of his current business because if he failed, he could easily bounce back with the help of his extensive network. He viewed his web of associates, peers, and clients as a giant safety net. It was like an insurance policy that allowed him to take risks in business. I've found that to be true myself. As I look back on my business ventures, I see that my failures may not have occurred, or might have been less damaging, if I'd had the right network at the time.

As you're planning your move from employee to owner, build a network you can rely on whether you stay in your current job or move out on your own. Build relationship capital within your work, adjunct to your work, or totally outside the scope of your job.

Remember the old adage that you are the sum of the people you spend the most time with. Your network will shape you. You will find mentors among your network. You will find opportunities in your network. The initial investment in a business often originates from an entrepreneur's network. Intentionally shaping your network is one of the quickest ways to rise out of your socioeconomic limitations.

In my first couple of business ventures, I had no mentors.

I made new mistakes every day and paid dearly for them. I was a business boy raised by wolves. It would be many years before I had met enough entrepreneurs to begin learning from other people's mistakes. It would be even longer before I found true mentors. Over the years, my network has been a place to vet ideas before making decisions. Those relationships have helped me avoid bad choices and bad investments multiple times. I've also found investors who have backed my deals, as well as people I've partnered with.

Network Up, Not Across

Unfortunately, those making the mental shift from employee to owner often begin with no understanding of networking. Employees may attend conferences and might learn a few things. Yet, they often miss the opportunity to intentionally connect with people who don't directly impact their current job. Some employees think of networking as an opportunity to score some facetime with the higher-ups, hoping that added visibility will give them an edge in getting a promotion or pay raise.

To be clear, this is not networking. It does little to increase your relationship capital. Networking is building a bank of relational currency you can draw from for the rest of your life. To view networking merely as associating only with people in your current role or pandering to your employer limits your growth in two ways.

Firstly, it limits your personal growth. You are shaped by

the people in your network. If those people are all the same as you in knowledge, experience, and job function, you won't learn much from them. You'll just spin your wheels along with others who are stuck. Your network should stretch you and expand your horizons. To do that, you need to get around people who are different from you, who know things you don't, and have experiences you haven't had.

Secondly, it gives you no new resources. An employee-style network doesn't allow you to find partners, investors, mentors, and collaborators. You need to level up your network if you want to go up in business. To go beyond where you are, you need a network that goes beyond your peers.

Be Generous and Reputable

A robust network is money in the bank. But here's where many people misunderstand and misuse their network. The currency of the network is reciprocity. That means you gain capital by contributing to your network. People who simply connect with others so they can ask questions or pitch ideas don't usually last long. Generosity is the secret to effective networking. Don't approach your network with your hands out. Go there to give. Learn what others need by taking a real interest in them and their ventures. Add value when you can. Start with curiosity, then deliver generosity. That's how you deposit capital in the networking bank.

There's one more often-overlooked aspect of networking that you must protect at all costs: your reputation. It's possible to have a vast network, be widely known, and even have contributed generously to the lives of others. Yet all of that will do little good if you are not seen as likable by others.

What is likeability? It's the feeling that you can be trusted. To provide value back to you, people in your network must feel favorably about you, which usually means they feel safe with you. In other words, they believe they can trust you.

Trust is built in several ways, most of which should seem obvious. We build trust when we honor our word, do what we say we are going to do, treat people with respect, refrain from gossiping, and speak honestly. Though obvious, these things are not always easy to do. They often come at a short-term cost.

Building trust also means avoiding things that ruin your reputation. Your likeability within your network is easily damaged by appearing to be cheap or taking short-term gains at the expense of long-term thinking. Nothing hurts a reputation more quickly than being always the taker but never the giver. Talking down to people or insulting them can do irreparable harm to a reputation.

So while it's true that your network is your greatest asset, this only remains true as long as your reputation is solid. Your ongoing contribution to that network as a curious and generous participant, combined with your reputation for trustworthiness, is money in the bank when it comes to upward movement.

One more note on integrity. As you keep your eye on the future, keep your feet in the present. Honor your present commitments as you build connections to draw on later. People who leave an employer on bad terms can squander relationship capital and lose their network. It is easy to get negative about the company, the boss, or the environment when you're in a job you don't like. Remember where we started: jobs suck. Yet maintaining integrity even as you swat flies will pay dividends down the road. Be prepared to leave at any time, and to do so on good terms.

Think Long-Term

Your reputation is a valuable asset but it's also illiquid. This means you can't necessarily cash it in right away. You'll build it for years before the dividends begin to flow your way. However, the beauty of a wide network and good reputation is that they provide a fertile ground for one of the most mysterious and precious experiences in both life and business—serendipity. Circumstances that many people chalk up to chance or a lucky break are often the product of the work they did many years ago.

I have been "blessed" with many opportunities that seemed to "fall into" my lap over the years. However, the seeds to those successes were sown years in advance. When someone calls me to say they have an opportunity to offer and I was the first one who popped into their mind, that's not chance. It's the result of something I did in the past that helped them, but didn't necessarily benefit me. Serendipity, that mysterious force that some of us seem to conjure at will, is merely an invisible thread connecting a moment in the past to the present time.

Flyswatting in Action

Relationships lead to reputation. And reputation invites opportunity. Connect with others who can help you get to where you want to go, and when the time comes, your reputation will precede you.

Give to others before asking for something in return. It really is true that "what goes around, comes around." It may take time and patience, but this is a tremendously more practical approach to life and work than the short-term "dog-eat-dog" approach that is especially popular in corporate America. Resist the temptation for short-term gain, and you'll stay in the game a lot longer.

Think of your reputation as a long-term investment in your success. Make careful but strategic deposits in your network and relationships on a regular basis, and do your best to act with integrity, respect, and honor. When people see this in you, they may not congratulate you at the time, but it's registering with them. And you never know when you'll need to access those deposits you've made in others.

VIII

THE PLAGUE

In the course of time, a terrible sickness passed through Namir. Thousands became ill and many died. The plague had not yet infected the palace, and the servants and guards were ordered to stay within the palace walls.

"We must protect the king's family," Rihat decreed.

Within a week, however, Rihat was taken ill with the plague and died. Kuri was appointed in his place, but he too developed a fever. Though he survived, he was confined to his quarters in quarantine. Anki, the wise old cook who had befriended Ubar, had become a trusted advisor to the king and recognized that the situation was grave. If the king were to continue hearing cases, he could be infected with the plague by a visitor to the court. If he suspended justice during his quarantine, the city would suffer further.

One day, Anki sent a message to Ubar through a merchant who delivered goods to the palace door. Ubar came to the palace in response to her summons.

"I have spoken with the king," Anki said. "I have advised that he not allow citizens to enter the court until the plague has passed."

Ubar nodded. "The king and his family should not be exposed."

"I agree," Anki continued, "but the king has refused. He believes suspending his judgments will put the city at further risk. And he is quite right."

Ubar said, "That is what makes him a great king, but it would not serve the kingdom well if he were to become ill. He is not a young man."

"Ah, that brings me to my point, Ubar," Anki said. "You are a young man and strong. I have suggested to the king that he allow you to hear the cases outside the main hall. Then you alone can come into the king's presence and relay the case to him for a decision."

"That would be an honor, but I am not worthy," Ubar said. "And I have only had two conversations with the king in my years . . . and they were only due to my mistake." Ubar's stomach lurched at the memory.

"You are the right person to do this, and I have convinced the king of it," Anki said. "I know that Yahatti had you listening to the king, and you will have his mind in your heart like no other."

Ubar was taken aback as he thought about this. Anki could see his concern and put her hand on his shoulder to reassure him.

"You have everything you need. In my estimation, you have heard more cases than anyone other than the king himself."

"No, many others know the king's mind better," Ubar exclaimed. "Think of Kuri. He has spent years at the king's side."

"Oh, no. On that point, you are wrong, Ubar. Both Rihat and Kuri were like so many other servants who do their jobs and nothing else, and tune everything else out. They never heard a single case, as you did not for your first few years. They have never awakened that part of the mind that you have. Thus, Kuri is not fit for the present task. I think you will see your knowledge at work in your new temporary role."

Ubar went home that night and discussed the matter with Bashaa.

"It is indeed a great honor," Bashaa said slowly. "But where is the profit in it? How much will this earn you?"

"There was no talk of gold," Ubar said. "I know that all who serve the king receive food and lodging, though little more."

"Hmm," Bashaa considered. "I have no advice for you, my son. I agree it is good to serve the king. Yet this will cost you many fine investment opportunities. You must do as you see fit."

Ubar did not sleep well that night. His mind was greatly troubled at the prospect before him. He knew that Bashaa was right, yet serving the king was both a great honor and opportunity. In the morning Ubar rose and walked resolutely to the palace. He entered the main hall where he met Anki, who ushered him to the king.

"I present your flymaster, my lord. You barely knew young Ubar, but he stood at your back longer than Yahatti sat in your presence as your scribe. Ubar is a keen observer and will relay your cases from a distance."

The king smiled. "I hope your plan works, Anki," he said. And to Ubar, "Now, let us see if you and I can keep business as usual for our fair city."

Anki led Ubar through the main doors into the outer hall where many people were seated around the walls or leaning against pillars.

Anki spoke loudly to the room, "As you know, I am Anki, the king's senior servant. The king has decreed that all cases be presented to Ubar, this young man, who will listen carefully and then return to the king to set forth your arguments. He will then return with the king's judgment."

A few in the room groaned. One voiced his objection, "Anki, we know you, but must we trust our lives and businesses to this former servant . . . a flyswatter no less?"

Anki raised both her hands.

"Friends, these are difficult times, I agree. But we cannot expose the king to the risks. I am too old to be put at risk as well. I trust Ubar beyond anyone I know, and I ask you to do the same. And some of you know him as a successful businessman who has seen the very types of disputes you bring to court for the king's judgment."

Ubar was surprised at this endorsement and felt very small and unworthy in the face of the objections.

The first case was presented, and Ubar listened attentively. He asked a few questions, which surprised the litigants a little. But they also took note that Ubar's questions seemed to show his understanding of their case. Ubar nodded and turned to the closed doors. Anki opened them and the two marched across the court to the king, who was eating grapes. The king was completely alone except for the young flyswatter, Lebashi, standing at his back, whisking with both hands and diligently doing his work.

Ubar found himself timid in the king's presence. Anki pushed Ubar forward a little bit and cleared her throat but did not speak. Ubar realized it was time to present the case and proceeded to recount it exactly as it was set forth. The king listened and then asked Ubar the very same questions that Ubar had asked the litigants. Ubar looked back at Anki as if to ask for a little help.

Anki spoke up, "My lord, your servant Ubar asked those very questions, which made me proud. I hope this shows that he is in tune with the king's mind."

The king laughed and said, "I am delighted. Please share their responses, Ubar!"

Ubar told the king the replies to his line of questioning.

The king pondered and then rendered a firm decision. Ubar and Anki returned to the outer hall. Ubar waited for Anki to announce the decision, but she nodded, indicating that he should speak. So, Ubar rendered the king's decision. The litigant who lost frowned but did not object. At that, Anki silently slipped out of the entry hall, leaving Ubar to hear the next case.

Ubar took his old room at the palace and continued to hear the king's cases each day. The work was challenging, but the stress diminished as he realized that the many cases he had seen and heard over the years made it easy for him to understand the issues, ask questions, and bring the king's decisions back to the litigants. The citizens did not object. In fact, they seemed to think that Ubar was an impartial listener and communicator.

Meanwhile, Kuri slowly became well and began to move about the palace. He had been trying to influence affairs from his quarantine without much success. He did not like the idea that a disgraced servant stood before the people as a mouthpiece for the king. One day, a servant quietly voiced his concern to Ubar.

"You are risking your neck, Ubar," he said. "You should let Kuri take over for you and return to normal life as soon as possible." Ubar understood that this message had come directly from Kuri himself. It was the same advice he had heard years before. Play it safe. Avoid risk. Do no more than you have to.

"Thank you for your advice," Ubar told the servant. "I will consider it carefully." Of course Ubar had no intention of resigning. He knew by now that Kuri and his ilk would always stand in the way of success. He would not be intimidated by them.

The next day, after Ubar presented a case to the king, the king paused for a moment. Before pronouncing a decision, he said, "Ubar, what decision do you think I would render in this case?"

Ubar was struck. He looked down and thought. His opinion was not important. But the king had asked what Ubar thought the *king's* decision would be, not his own.

"My lord, I believe you would find for the plaintiff," Ubar replied.

"You are correct. That is what I would rule. Now what would you rule, Ubar?"

Ubar paused, not really wanting to respond to such a bold question. Yet he dared not refuse to answer the king.

"I would find for the plaintiff as well," said Ubar.

"Why?" asked the king.

"I am not completely sure, my king, but I think it is due to the credibility of her story. I think my mind is making judgments that are not easy to put into words. I am comparing the case to dozens of others that have been before you."

The king seemed pleased and broke into a grin.

"I think you have done well to listen and build your intuition. Yes, the facts are clear, as they usually are. But gut knowledge comes only from having observed many men and women tell their stories and make their cases."

Ubar paused, as if to say something. The king prodded him to speak.

"My lord, I have learned something about the mind that I cannot clearly explain. It feels to me that my mind has reached its limit when I learn new information. Yet the next day, it is as if there is room for more. The more I fill my mind, the more empty space is discovered."

The king was pleased with Ubar's forthrightness and impressed with his wisdom.

"You have learned one of the most valuable lessons in life, Ubar. You are correct that your capacity for knowledge grows with knowledge itself. Most people learn only the minimum necessary to do their job at its most basic level."

Ubar listened attentively and nodded.

"True wisdom comes when you realize that you will never fill your mind completely. As you say, there is always room for more learning. Even if you were to attain the enlightenment of Anu today, you would have room for more by tomorrow."

Ubar nodded. "Thank you for listening to me and teaching me, my king."

Ubar returned to his post at the great doors and heard his next case.

In the coming weeks, the king began to play a little game with Ubar. When Ubar would present a case, the king would ask Ubar how he would decide. Ubar would explain his judgment, then the king would nod and say, "That is my judgment as well." The king never found fault with Ubar's judgment and only a few times asked him to make further arguments for his position.

After several months, the plague subsided. Ubar expected to be sent home. He was weary of the sense that his fellow servants were jealous of his position. Worse, he was still wary of Kuri, who continued to look for opportunities to discredit him.

Anki understood Ubar's stress, yet she was eager to further deploy his wisdom for the king's benefit. Anki asked Ubar to come with her after breakfast one day. She led him to the king's personal study, where he seemed to expect their visit.

Anki spoke, "My lord, have you considered our discussion further?"

"Yes," said the king. "I am reluctant, Anki. Giving up my role as judge may disconnect me from the people and jeopardize the city's wellbeing."

Ubar looked at Anki in surprise.

"You will still be judge, my king," Anki said. "But you will hear only appeals. You can attend some of the regular court hearings if you choose, to ensure the citizens feel you are aware of all things in your kingdom."

"I think it is now or never," said the king, and he turned his gaze to Ubar.

"Ubar," said the king, "I would like you to continue serving me as you have been. I decree you Judge of First Instance. You will decide all cases in my court, though I will allow citizens to appeal to me in certain instances."

Ubar's mouth hung open, his eyes wide.

"Do not be surprised, my son," the king said. "You have proven yourself these past few months. And Anki is right. At my age, I cannot hear cases day after day. Besides that, the city is prosperous. There are ceremonies and celebrations to attend. I can now take time to enjoy them."

The king looked directly at Ubar.

"You are the only person qualified to stand in my place. Will you serve the kingdom in this way?"

Ubar almost fainted. His mind raced with thoughts. How had he, an orphan servant boy, risen to such a place in the kingdom? He breathed evenly and came back to his senses.

"I will do as my lord wishes," Ubar said. "Whether swatting flies or making judgments." Here Ubar paused, realizing he was about to make a bold request. "I have only one favor to ask of the king," he said.

"You have only to name it," the king replied.

"I ask that your flyswatter, Lebashi, be placed in my service."

The king smiled a knowing smile.

"It is done," he said.

Over the coming years, Ubar used all the wisdom he

learned by watching the king to become a very wise judge. Even those whom he decided against respected him.

The king heard appeals once each week, and rarely found fault with Ubar's decisions. This brought continued confidence throughout the city. Ubar enjoyed an honored place among the servants. And each day he sat in the outer hall, hearing cases brought by the people. And each day Lebashi stood behind Ubar, deftly swatting any fly that threatened to land on the Judge of First Instance.

PRINCIPLE #8

YOU CAN LEARN, OR YOU CAN EARN.

Some people see their careers as a means to an end—a series of progressive steps they have to take in hopes that all this hard work will pay off some day. And then, at a certain point, they get to where they think they want to go and then settle. This can be an unfulfilling and ultimately unwise way to live, because it assumes the permanence of your current circumstance which is never true. Nothing lasts forever, and the more you try to hold on to something, the easier it often slips through your fingers.

Still, many people work jobs they hate to make money that hopefully allows them to do the things they love. It's a familiar story to most people. But why do so many of us do this to ourselves? Well, first, it's all most of us know; and second, there's some truth to it. To be blunt, this approach *works*, at least to an extent. You can, in fact, kill yourself at a career you loathe, putting in the hours, days, and years to get ahead and—if you're lucky—eventually cash it all in for fifteen to twenty years of the "good life." But what will that have cost you? It's no small exaggeration to say most of your life.

Most employees prioritize earning over learning, and as a result handcuff themselves into situations that, as they get older, are nearly inescapable. As a young lawyer, I saw this unfold before me a number of times. Getting their start at the firm, ambitious new lawyers would work long, thankless hours, putting their time in to make a name for themselves. Then, some of them would make partner, at which point they'd put their careers on autopilot and let the younger attorneys do the grunt work while they cruised to retirement.

It's certainly an attractive path, but it comes with its own glass ceiling. When you spend decades grinding it out to get to a place of complacency, there really is nowhere else to go. You're stuck at this point. This is the path of Rihat and Kuri, who saw their jobs as the ultimate destination instead of yet another opportunity to learn and grow. It's no wonder they were so jealous of their turf—it was all they had.

As a young lawyer, I knew I had to pick a lane in my own career. By that I don't mean a legal specialty, but a pathway to success. Would I focus on learning or earning? Both had their risks, but one seemed to clearly have greater potential payoff down the line. Would I follow the way of Rihat and so many of the older attorneys, working hard for a few years with the goal of getting a promotion and milking that salary for years? Or would I follow the Way of the Flyswatter and eventually venture out on my own, shedding the golden handcuffs in favor of a life of freedom and adventure? I knew that's what I wanted, but it also terrified me. What would happen if I burned my bridges as an employee but later needed to return?

While I was contemplating making a move, a mentor showed me how wrong this thinking was, telling me that my experience as an entrepreneur would make me more valuable as an employee, not less. Regardless of the outcome of my venture, I'd be in a stronger position than before by virtue of my knowledge and experience. That advice helped inspire me to eventually make my exit from the law firm to start my own practice. It was a small but right step in my eventual journey to ultimate freedom and independence.

Employment Is Always an Option

When you follow the Way of the Flyswatter, you have the agency to weave in and out of employment whenever you need to or want to. It's foolish to believe that sticking it out in a job you dislike for twenty or thirty years will bring you greater security. You may work a job in exchange for a paycheck only to find yourself forced out by a reorganization, change of ownership, or some unexpected market volatility. Coasting for five or ten years will do nothing to prepare you for that reality and may cost you more in the long run. What could you have done with that time if you had been preparing for your next move?

As a flyswatter, the primary opportunity you are always seeking is to learn new skills, develop yourself, and build your network. In a certain sense, having a job sucks, compared to the freedom you'll experience as your own employer. But there are ways to enjoy our current circumstances while we are preparing for what's to come, even if we don't know what it is.

Like most people, you probably want to work for yourself, control more of your time, make the most money possible, and live the life you want. A job will never give you this kind of opportunity, at least not compared to what you can create for yourself. But it doesn't have to be all or nothing. The Way of the Flyswatter suggests that you use your job as an opportunity to help you acquire the tools you need to eventually get the life you want. It's possible to have your cake and eat it, too.

Your employer may never know, or even care, that your end goal is to get out of this job. Frankly, it's none of their concern. So long as you do the job you have, who cares what your motives are? This, unlike the fledgling lawyer jockeying for partner so they can soon hit easy street, is an ultimately fulfilling endeavor, because it involves new challenges, everyday on-the-job learning, and personal growth that brings with it regular rewards.

When you take this approach to your job, the reality is that you'll probably become a star employee—as is often the case for flyswatters—because you are doing more for seemingly no reason. You may even get promoted or get an unexpected raise as a result of your performance. You might become head of your division or department or be asked to train your peers. These are all signs that you are on the right track—not to get a lofty position at the company where you can start coasting, but setting yourself up for even greater freedom.

Nonetheless, when you get these opportunities, take them. They will advance your exit plan by giving you new opportunities to learn and grow, expanding your network and improving your income as you move closer and closer to your exit.

Beware the Temptation to Settle

Be careful on this new path. Promotions and praise can become traps for would-be entrepreneurs, landing you in a place that you never intended. As I mentioned earlier, it's easy to get sucked into the honey trap of ladder climbing. You may come to feel so locked into your salary and benefits that you abandon your dream of entrepreneurship altogether. This is common and not necessarily wrong.

If, in this process of becoming a flyswatter, you decide that what you ultimately want is a cushy job, then by all means stay there. But if such ascents merely put you into a place of greater fear of losing what you have, just know that you have options. The goal of a flyswatter is never to get to a really good job and stay put. The goal is to learn and grow and use those competencies and connections to buy yourself more freedom.

Flyswatters don't always follow a linear path on their journey to ownership. Ubar certainly didn't when he was let go from the palace or when he gave up self-employment to move back to the palace. When planning your exit, be on alert for all opportunities to learn and network, even those that don't involve a promotion or raise. Salary fixation has cost many would-be entrepreneurs a golden opportunity.

I've seen this happen a number of times, once when I was involved in recruiting a potential flyswatter. We were hiring for a managerial position at a company where I worked as a general manager. It was an important role, and one that would provide a pathway to advancement for anyone who was skilled in that particular trade but not yet trained as a manager. The base pay was about $90,000 per year, plus a meaningful bonus opportunity.

There was one hitch. The ideal candidates for the position were highly skilled tradespeople. That meant they were near the top of the ladder in compensation for their skill. So moving out of the field and into an entry-level management position would actually be a move down the pay scale for them. That's not an uncommon situation. In the process of switching ladders you sometimes lose a rung or two. Moving from the labor force to the management team is a boost in responsibility, but it can initially be a step down in terms of pay.

For aspiring entrepreneurs, the trade-off can be totally worthwhile. In management, they gain visibility into what other managers do, and they can acquire the skills required to move higher in leadership. They participate in goal setting and planning. They work on budgets. They learn the tools that entrepreneurs need. Few companies will hire a new manager at high pay, given how much training they require and how new managers often produce mediocre results until they have become fully competent.

Of course, not everyone has the mind of a flyswatter. What I found in interviewing for this role was that most candidates could not grasp the value of the opportunity presented to them. All they could think about was the pay. It was a bit like interviewing Rihat or Kuri. Many candidates had the same mindset of complacency and self-protection. Several were almost rude about being asked to take a role that was as a step down in pay.

I tried to explain that once they mastered the job, they would be able to move into the operations manager and general manager positions at much higher pay. And their experience would be transferable to other jobs, other industries, or even self-employment. Most couldn't grasp that. Their only concept of advancement was to earn just a little more than they were currently making.

One candidate stands out in my mind as a hard resistor. He was a seasoned field supervisor and already understood the business quite well. Within a short time he could have been on track for a position like operations manager or branch manager. First, he would have to learn the basics of management, such as controlling cost, purchasing, and working with vendors. He also needed to learn people management skills like leading a team, tracking time, handling payroll, and employment law.

The problem was that he didn't know what he didn't know. He had no idea of the range of issues he would have to deal with as a manager. When I tried to explain this, it was as if I were speaking another language. He couldn't see the gaps in his knowledge and skill, and couldn't appreciate what he could gain—even if this meant a slightly lower rate of pay.

At the end of the negotiation, we were less than $10,000 away from what he wanted. Yet, he refused the job. Our hiring team was confounded because we knew this was the only path for a person in his position to become a professional manager. He was so stuck on his belief that he deserved a higher salary, even as a brand-new manager, that he was willing to stay in a job that had absolutely no potential growth. For him, money was more important than opportunity, which is a bit short-sighted considering true opportunity always leads to more money.

How to Hire a Flyswatter

Most of what we've learned so far has applied to employees who aspire to be owners. There's another lesson here, and that's for anyone who is an owner looking to acquire the best employees. Never hire Kuri if you can hire Ubar. In fact, never hire Kuri at all.

Recruit and promote people who are interested in their own growth. They'll serve you the best in the long run, even if some leave the company. Even large organizations should embrace the Way of the Flyswatter; to hire and grow employees who may have ambitions of self-employment. The companies who are bold enough to do this will get the benefit of ambitious employees, and some will stay and make a career out of their job even if others find their way to greener pastures.

A case in point is the candidate I just mentioned. Based on our interaction, we learned he wasn't the right person for leadership because he had no more vision for himself or the company than to make an incremental gain. Even if we'd found a way to up the salary by $10,000, we would have been disappointed. He would forever have the *employee mentality*, trading time for money, rather than seeing his role as a training ground for becoming a professional manager.

I could give you countless examples of this phenomenon, like Jennifer, the senior manager I once hired who had all the right qualifications on paper, but who had never taken the time to learn more than her job. When promoted, she floundered because she didn't know the first thing about the operation of a department she'd worked in for years. When asked why she didn't know how to perform certain functions, she said, "Nobody ever showed me what to do."

If you have this mentality, you'll probably never make it out there in entrepreneur land. It's up to you—not your employer—to seek opportunities at your job. No one is coming to save you. Your company is not likely to set you on a pathway to achieve the competence you need to be self-employed. Most companies don't even do a good job at helping employees prepare for the next job within the company. Those who take their flyswatting seriously will find ways to learn that prepare them for an upward career move more than those who wait for the company to train them.

Every Job Is Preparation for the Next

Good companies promote not based on how well you do your current job, but on how well you're prepared for the next one.[4] That means *everyone* should follow the Way of the Flyswatter. Whether you want to move from employee to entrepreneur or rise within your current company, it is the job you have that prepares you for the next one. Many people find themselves with seniority, but without readiness. To be unprepared is to be powerless.

That means every flyswatter is really self-employed. Wherever you are, and whatever you're doing, think like an owner. You work for you, even while you appear to be working for your employer. Take full responsibility for your future by taking responsibility for your present. We are all, actually, flyswatters.

Flyswatting in Action

When you focus on the benefits of the job itself, you miss the benefit of learning. Don't let the promise of any position distract you from the possibility of what you ultimately want and deserve—which is more freedom.

No job is irreplaceable. You can move in and out of employment (or different roles) if you choose to. Becoming a flyswatter gives you the most options possible, including entrepreneurship as well as the option for potential employment at any point, should you need it.

As a flyswatter, be alert for learning opportunities that may not include promotion and may even pay less. You can learn, or you can earn. But often, you have to choose between the two. Just know which one you are picking.

IX

REVENGE OF THE FLYSWATTERS

For three years Ubar served as King Tattannu's Judge of First Instance. Within the first year, the number of appeals taken to the king slowed to a trickle. Tattannu now held court only one day a month, and even then he seldom heard more than one or two cases. Namir continued to prosper as the king, now in his seventieth year, was able to spend nearly all of his time inspecting the kingdom and consulting with the great people of the city.

After one of his monthly court sessions, the king consulted with Ubar, as was his practice.

"You have become an excellent judge," the king said. "It appears that I can be replaced after all."

Ubar's eyes rose in alarm.

"No, my king!" he nearly shouted. "Your people need you. I am no substitute for your divine presence in our land."

"Relax, my son," the king chuckled. "It is a good thing that I can be replaced. This has freed me to do even more for my kingdom. We were a fair and just society when I held court each day. Since I have been able to attend to other matters of state, we are expanding beyond our borders with trade and influence. Namir grows only greater."

Ubar sighed in relief.

"Now I will promote you again, Ubar," the king said. "You will be my Minister of Justice. I will no longer hear cases, even appeals. I appoint you to oversee all legal matters in Namir. You will train a Judge of First Instance. Or more than one if you like. They can take your place in the outer court, and you can hear appeals in my place."

Ubar was no longer surprised when opportunities came to him. He still felt unworthy to stand in the king's place, yet he knew that anxiety was to be expected when taking on new responsibility.

"I serve at the king's pleasure," Ubar said, "as always."

"Excellent," the king said. "I will announce your appointment immediately."

Within a month, Ubar had instituted the king's desired changes. In a move that surprised many in the palace, Ubar appointed two Judges of First Instance. The first was the door administrator who had heard Ubar's case against the fraudulent trader all those years ago. Ubar knew that he understood the basic tenets of the law very well, so he handled all matters involving property claims of less than one day's wages. That accounted for the majority of claims among small merchants and landowners. In effect, Ubar created a small claims court. Cases could still be appealed, but Ubar knew it would be rare for such small amounts.

The other Judge of First Instance would hear all cases involving claims of more than one day's wages, and any cases involving crimes against a person. Though these cases were fewer in number, Ubar knew that they were far more complex. For this position, Ubar selected Lebashi, his flyswatter.

"Me?" Lebashi said, nearly dumbfounded. "No, my lord, I could not stand in judgment. I am only a flyswatter."

Ubar smiled. "No, Lebashi, you have never been just a flyswatter. For four years you stood beside the king, listening to every word he said—and I know that Anki questioned you each week about cases, just as I have done these past three years."

"That is true," Lebashi said, "yet there is still much I don't know."

"You know more than you realize," Ubar said. "And don't be afraid to rely on your instincts."

Lebashi still seemed hesitant.

"Listen," Ubar said. "You will start out as I started, listening to cases and relaying the details to me. That will give you the confidence to begin making judgments on your own."

Lebashi agreed, and the new system of justice worked well for all of Namir.

However, not everyone was delighted with the new arrangement. As usual, Kuri and his minions in the palace were irate.

"You should have been Minister of Justice," friends whispered to Kuri. "Enough of these flyswatters!"

"They refuse to know their place," Kuri agreed. "But we shall see about that."

Kuri seethed with resentment against Anki, Lebashi, and anyone associated with Ubar. Knowing Ubar carried too much favor with the king to be attacked directly, Kuri hatched a plot against Anki. He planned to whittle away at the "flyswatters," as he called them, and restore his authority within the palace.

Kuri and his cabal of angry servants decided to stage a false accusation against Anki, spreading rumors that she was using her influence within the palace to gain financial profit. Like little butterflies, they began to circulate among the palace staff and in the marketplace, claiming that she had business dealings with powerful and wealthy men in the city. Eventually, the rumor reached Bashaa, who kept track of nearly all happenings of the city.

Bashaa, concerned about the damage this report could do—whether or not it was true—asked for an audience with the king. Remembering Bashaa's brother, Yahatti, the king agreed to meet.

"My lord," said Bashaa. "I hear a vicious rumor that your steward Anki is using her power for her own ends."

The king replied, "And you come to me to accuse her?"

"Of course not, my lord. In fact, I must say that I have no direct evidence. I know only that Anki holds great influence in the palace, and that my dear brother Yahatti trusted her deeply."

"So, you believe the rumors are false?" asked the king.

"I cannot say," Bashaa said. "But I know they can do great damage to your royal authority, whether true or false. I believe the king should investigate and render his wise judgment."

"Thank you, Bashaa," King Tattannu replied. "Indeed, rumors are like cancer and must be cut out quickly or they bring much destruction."

The king called for Lebashi, and the two developed a plan. They were both keen to find the source of the rumor and wanted to cut it out decisively.

A few days later, Kuri was summoned to the king's court. When he arrived, Anki was on her knees with two guards beside her, both armed with swords.

Kuri was pleased to think his plan was working.

"Yes, my lord?" he said as he bowed before the king.

"Kuri," said the king. "There is a rumor that my faithful servant Anki has wielded her influence to gain a personal fortune. Have you heard this as well?"

"Yes. Unfortunately, my lord, I have," said Kuri.

The king stroked his beard and thought as he looked at Kuri.

"I am inclined to pass judgment here today, Kuri," the king said. "Death is the penalty for such conduct, is it not?"

"It is, my lord," replied Kuri. Realizing his plot was working perfectly, he did his best not to overplay his hand.

"Lebashi," the king said, and Lebashi stepped forward.

"You are the Judge of First Instance for crimes against people," the king continued. "Is there a punishment for making false witness?"

Lebashi replied, "Yes, my king. The punishment is death."

"Why is the punishment so harsh?" the king asked.

"If people lied with impunity, they would lie for their own gain," Lebashi responded. "That would be the same as stealing from the king."

Kuri was confused by this discussion, but waited patiently, knowing Anki would soon be out of his way.

Now the king addressed the entire court.

"Does anyone present have evidence to show that Anki has committed a misdeed?"

No one spoke.

Breaking the silence, Kuri offered, "My king, the absence of witnesses does not prove that Anki has not profited in your service."

"That is true," the king said. "But we must also establish that the report is true, not false." At this he addressed the court again. "Does anyone have evidence that the report against Anki is false?"

Silence fell on the court. After several moments, a servant girl came out from behind a group of courtesans. She bowed. Kuri grew pale as he realized it was one of the kitchen maids who had plotted with him to spread the rumor.

"I do, my lord," she said timidly. "I was part of a meeting with other servants who discussed creating a false rumor against Anki."

Kuri began to sweat.

The king rose up in anger, shouting, "Who would do such a thing, girl? Tell me now!"

The young woman paused, tearing up, and said, "I am responsible and others too, my king. Our leader was Kuri, the king's servant."

Kuri looked for an escape, but guards were everywhere. He sank to his knees before the king.

"My lord, I desired only to protect you and the kingdom from those who seek to rise up and be greater than the king."

"Release Anki!" shouted the king. Anki stood and bowed to the king without a word.

"Is there any defense that anyone wishes to lodge for Kuri?" asked the king.

Silence fell over the room. Kuri began to sob at the king's feet. At last, a voice was heard from the back of the court.

"I will speak."

All eyes turned to see who would speak in Kuri's defense. Striding toward the king's throne was none other than Ubar.

"My lord," Ubar began, "Kuri has indeed plotted evil

against Anki and against the kingdom. His false report could have cost lives. His own life, by law, is now forfeit." Ubar paused to look about the room. "He should be punished, no doubt. But I ask the king to impose a punishment other than death."

"You are my Minister of Justice," the king said. "Would you not uphold the law?"

Ubar replied, "As I have so often heard the king say, the purpose of the law is twofold. It is first to bring justice, and second to instruct the people." Here Ubar made a bow before King Tattannu. "I am confident our wise ruler can fashion a sentence that does both."

The king nodded slowly, deep in thought. He remained so for several minutes. At last, he spoke.

"Here is my judgment," he said slowly. "Kuri, you wanted to advance your place in the king's service. Your jealousy led you to despise anyone who showed initiative or ambition. For years you have given only the barest effort required of you, and you expected others to do the same."

Kuri had stopped sobbing, but continued to cower before the king.

"And here is your reward," the king said. "I promote you to dung shoveler, and I decree that shall be your position for life. You will report immediately to the Dung Master at the city gate. Each day you will walk the streets shoveling the excrement left behind by livestock. I am confident there is no place where less will be required of you."

Snickers rippled through the court.

"As for the rest," the king declared. "Lebashi will conduct an investigation to determine who took part in this plot. They shall be banished from the palace. They shall be given employment as flyswatters in the fields and construction sites of the kingdom. From there, their fate shall be in their own hands."

Later, when the court had cleared, the king spoke to Anki.

"I never doubted you, Anki. You are my most loyal servant."

"Thank you, my king," Anki replied. "Your judgment today was wise and fair. With the cancer eliminated, the kingdom will prosper even more than before. You are still the wisest man in all of Namir."

"Perhaps so," the king said. "But not by much . . . and not for long."

Anki's expression narrowed in concern.

The king smiled. "Kings are mortal," he said. "Even those descended from the gods." As he rose to leave the royal court, Anki noticed a hesitation in the king's step.

PRINCIPLE #9

GIVERS GAIN, TAKERS LOSE.

The Way of the Flyswatter involves learning, growing, building relationships, planning, and taking risks when necessary. It also involves generosity. Think of Yahatti, plucking young Ubar from servitude in Bashaa's household. There was far less to be gained by Yahatti than by Ubar. Yet, the older man understood the value in employing any enterprising young person, so he gave Ubar a chance. That eventually paid great dividends for both Yahatti and the kingdom.

Ubar followed the same route. Once a flyswatter, he became a trainer of flyswatters. He developed an eye for talent, which led him to employ Lebashi. That relationship profited both of them.

This is always the way. Learning, growing, and helping others succeed is the surest path to finding success for yourself. Consider your entrepreneurial path a journey. On that journey, you'll succeed most when you create opportunities for others as well as for yourself. Flyswatters are givers. They give outstanding service to their employers. They share learning and ideas with others. They create opportunity for themselves, and that creates opportunity for others. Givers gain.

Flyswatter Becomes the Master

After leaving the law firm to open my own practice, I began to build a staff. That involved hiring clerks, who are generally lawyers in training, fresh out of law school and looking for on-the-job experience before taking the bar exam. It didn't take me long to figure out that some were young Ubars, others were modern-day Kuris. I diligently screened and carefully selected the best candidates I could.

One year, just after I'd hired a fresh crop of clerks, a young law student named Kayla came to see me. Kayla was bright and eager, and she practically begged for clerkship. I thought she had potential, but I'd already hired all the staff my business plan called for. I hated telling her no, but I didn't want to overextend myself financially, especially since my practice was relatively new. But Kayla wouldn't take no for an answer. She offered to work on pro bono cases at no pay, just for the opportunity to do some real lawyering.

"Are you sure you want to do that?" I asked her. The last thing I wanted was to bring on an employee on a no-fee basis, only to have them become frustrated at the arrangement after a few months.

But Kayla was nothing if not positive, and she said she'd be delighted for the opportunity. Based on that assurance, I gave her a chance.

I could immediately tell it was the right decision. Kayla proved to be a quick learner and was always eager for greater opportunities, despite the fact that she was giving away her time. She did a great job for the firm and the pro bono clients. And I could see by her relentless curiosity that she was getting "paid" in knowledge and experience rather than money.

When the year was up, Kayla left to work for another law firm. She continued to gain experience, and easily passed the bar exam. After that, she returned to me, asking for a job.

I was eager to take her on, but I lacked the room in my small firm. Again, we reached an agreement that was not ideal for Kayla, but which kept her engaged and learning. She agreed to work for one-third of her billing, meaning she'd earn just 33 percent of what I charged clients for her services. It was the best I could offer, and she was willing.

Again, Kayla set out to gain all she could from the experience. She stuck to me closer than Ubar clung to King

Tattannu, listening and observing as I directed the firm. I knew she was becoming a fine lawyer. More than that, I began to think she could one day become a partner, either here or at another law firm.

Some time later, I was preparing for a sabbatical, which meant spending several months out of the country. I briefly considered inviting Kayla to manage the firm in my absence, but concluded she was not quite ready. I called her in to tell her that I'd be handing over the firm to someone else for a time. I said I knew she would be disappointed. By now, I should have anticipated that she'd come back at me with an alternative plan.

"How about this," she said. "Take your sabbatical, and let me run the firm while you're gone. If you can be available for questions just one hour a day, I know I can do this."

"Actually," I said, "that just might work." We decided to give it a try.

After months of living in Bali and working only one hour a day, I realized the practice was running better than ever, all thanks to Kayla and my long-time paralegal Jess. She had proved that she could do the job of running the firm and had learned to be the responsible partner. Not long after coming back from Bali, I made her a partner.

Over the next few years, I pushed more and more responsibility Kayla's way and enjoyed seeing her grow even as my role diminished. With the extra time in my schedule, I taught law at both San Diego law schools and helped direct law clinical programs there. I also published the first casebook on trademark prosecution. Although it is by no means the best piece of academic work in the field, it is my contribution. And teaching for a decade was a way of contributing something to the future of the legal profession. My freedom to teach and contribute to aspiring lawyers was possible only because Kayla had moved beyond swatting flies.

I did continue to work in the practice part-time, meeting frequently with Kayla to iron out any problems that developed. It was a busy season, and Kayla continued learning through the challenges. When things would get hectic, I waved an arm expansively around the conference room and said, "Someday, Kayla, all of this will be yours!" We would both laugh, but I wasn't joking. I knew it was my destiny to move on and hers was to stay with the practice.

Eventually, the time came when I was ready for another big change. I had done all I could with my practice, and more than I ever expected with my law career. When this time came, Kayla and I struck a deal, and she acquired my practice. The young flyswatter had now become the master.

Stepping Aside to Let Others Shine

At some point you, like Ubar, will have opportunities to bring others along on the journey. Invest in them, just as others invested in you. Keep your eye out for eager, high-performing people. Bring them into your network. Become the mentor to them that others were to you. Yahatti trained Ubar, Ubar trained Lebashi, and on it goes.

This cycle works in reverse too, so beware. Those who take but don't give, fill only the minimum requirements, or become a drain on your efforts. Probably the starkest contrast I've seen between a genuine flyswatter and a complacent complainer was between two employees who worked in the same department of a business I managed: Ron and Rose.

Ron managed the department and had a good deal of seniority in the company. Up to that point, he'd had the career trajectory of someone who would be in line for the general manager's role. His department was doing okay, but he more or less did just what was expected of him and not much more. Though he was underperforming, Ron would complain that his talent was being wasted. He believed he was general manager material, and probably should have been promoted already. So when the GM spot came up, Ron expected to waltz into the role.

That didn't happen.

Instead the job went to Rose, who had been working in Ron's department. She was an administrator with no experience in the technical side of the business. She dealt with customers, scheduled technicians, filed permits, and registered equipment, but had no field experience. She had a fairly good job and could have let it go at that. But Rose did more.

While doing her own job, she learned her boss's job as well. She understood how to manage the department, handle the budget and staff, and everything that goes into being a manager. That didn't go unnoticed. In fact, nobody was surprised when Rose was promoted over Ron. Well, nobody but Ron. Like Ubar, Rose had been listening in on the business all those years. Ron was like Kuri, expecting to be honored for his seniority and rewarded for his many years of coasting. Having shown no entrepreneurial spirit in his current job, his employers were not about to trust him with even more responsibility.

Years ago, I heard this bit of advice: A-level leaders hire A-level employees; B-level leaders hire C-level employees. Be the best, most eager, forward-thinking, inquisitive, responsibility-taking flyswatter you can be. You'll find that like-minded people are willing to join you and you won't be intimidated by their desire to achieve. But the moment you begin to hoard your resources, guard your position, and view others as potential threats, that momentum will shift. Givers gain, takers lose.

That, too, is the Way of the Flyswatter.

Flyswatting in Action

Givers gain. When the opportunity arises to help someone else shine, seize it for all it's worth, because such a move will not only help someone else out; it will free up your time to do more of what you love.

Takers lose. When you hoard the influence and opportunity you have, withholding it from other eager flyswatters, you are often seen as miserly and selfish. This is not the kind of person others want to help. What you have will eventually be taken from you. The only way to get more is to give what you have away, especially when it comes to influence.

Flyswatters surround themselves with like-minded people. Find the best, most motivated people you can work with and do everything you can to help them get what they want. Then, trust the process.

X

THE STORY CONTINUES

For several weeks after the plotters were expelled, Anki continued to observe the king's movements. His step continued to slow, and she noticed that his wit was not quite as sharp as before. One day after consulting with the city's leading traders, the king stood to leave the court, wavered on his feet for a moment, then collapsed.

Taken to his bed, he spoke with difficulty and could not lift his right arm. The king called for his senior counselors, including Anki and Ubar.

"My days are coming to an end," he said with slurred speech. "Anu has revealed that I will cross the Great River very soon."

"No, master," some said quietly, though all knew it was true. Anki sobbed gently, and Ubar wiped a tear from his eyes.

"My son and heir, Prince Abdili, is just eight years old. He is not ready to rule. Therefore, I decree that Ubar, my faithful Minister of Justice, shall be Grand Vizier and shall manage my kingdom in trust for the prince."

Ubar could barely choke out his reply, "I serve at my king's pleasure," he said, "as always."

That night, King Tattannu quietly slipped into the presence of Anu.

"This whisk is very broad with a bushy tail," Ubar said. "What do you suppose it is good for?"

"It must be used for broad strokes," Abdili said. "You could never strike a single fly with it."

"Excellent," said Ubar. "And what about this lash?"

"Ah," Abdili said, "I think that you could strike a single fly from the air six feet away."

"Quite right," said Ubar. "Here, you try it."

Seated on a chair in the center of the room was a young servant, flies buzzing around his head. The lash snapped. "Ouch!" he cried.

"A thousand pardons," Abdili said. "I am still quite clumsy." The boy smiled.

"You do well for a beginner," Ubar said. "Now I leave you to your teacher, who will complete your training."

Lebashi stepped forward. "Thank you, Vizier," he said. "Come, Prince. We have much work to do."

For nine years, Ubar ruled Namir as Grand Vizier. Lebashi, now Minister of Justice, supervised Prince Abdili's training, first as flyswatter, then clerk, then Judge of First Instance, and finally as Lebashi's replacement as Minister of Justice.

Through the years, Namir prospered greatly. Many traders arrived from the Far East, the Greeklands, Egypt, and India, bringing wine, spices, and fabrics, and enriching Namir with gold. The city gained such renown that some began to call it "Gateway to the Gods," which translates to "Babylon."

At last, Prince Abdili attained his seventeenth year and was prepared for coronation. He had learned every aspect of the kingdom, from the lowliest servant's job to the ministry of justice, trading policy, and the administration of wealth. Though young, he was indeed ready to rule.

On the eve of his coronation, the young prince summoned his Grand Vizier for a final interview.

"You have taught me much, Ubar," the prince said. "I feel as though I have been schooled by the wisest man in Babylon."

"That would be your father, my prince," Ubar said. "King Tattannu was wise beyond compare."

"A wise response," the prince said. "Tell me, Ubar, will you continue to serve my kingdom as Minister of Justice? Or Minister of Trade, perhaps?"

"I think not, kind prince," Ubar said. "I am humbled by your trust, yet I have had another idea in mind."

"Oh?"

"Yes, my lord. I have for some time been considering a venture into the cattle market."

"The cattle market?" the prince asked in surprise. "Ubar, forgive me, but in all our years together I have never once heard you mention cattle. What do you know about trading livestock?"

"Nothing, my lord."

"Then how do you propose to succeed in this venture? I know that you are a man of some means, but you cannot expect to succeed with gold alone. Where will you even begin?"

"My prince, I have heard that Elishu, the renowned cattle trader from Namir, is in need of a flyswatter. I will begin there."

PRINCIPLE #10

WE ARE ALL UBAR.

Over the years, I had been involved with an embarrassing number of failed business ventures. Their worthless stock certificates would be enough to paper my office walls, had I the desire to do so. Along the way, I also had some good runs in business and real estate. But I wanted to go deeper as an entrepreneur and business operator. I wanted to learn new things, expand as an investor, and even learn how to do a "real job" if necessary. Leaving law was not retirement. It was the beginning of a new path, putting all my attention into business and exiting law as a profession.

As I prepared to hand off the law practice to Kayla, I'd been watching business listings to see what I might acquire. I didn't have a particular industry in mind, but I liked the idea of buying a business that was low-tech and involved a staple product or service. This was right about the time when many baby boomers were retiring and selling their businesses, so there were numerous opportunities that lined up with my goals. One was a plumbing and HVAC business. The owner was ready to retire, and it was the exact type of business I'd been hunting for.

In my network, there was one obvious person to ask for advice. Ken Goodrich had come into my life through happenstance. He was the force behind one of the fastest growing HVAC companies in the country, and I chanced to meet him by stepping onto his private jet. I had been invited as part of a small entourage with Michael E. Gerber, the world's number one small business guru and author of the book *The E-Myth*. Michael was being air chauffeured to speak at a conference, and I was along for the ride. Ken was magnetic, and he and I ended up talking about life and business over the next few days. So when I ran across the opportunity to buy a plumbing and HVAC business a few months later, I called him for advice.

Ken volunteered to come in person, meet the seller, and help me ask questions. After the meeting, we made our way to a cigar bar in San Diego's Old Town. Ken was pensive for a while, but eventually started a discussion about the meeting.

"That's a fine little business," Ken said. "You've done well on setting up the deal structure."

I nodded. "Thanks."

He puffed on the cigar, then said, "I've got a better idea though." He looked directly at me. "How about you come work for us?"

I probably looked a bit surprised. Fortunately, Ken went on. "We'll show you all the things you would have done wrong, plus you'll make some money when we sell the business. After that, if we can keep working together, great. If not, you'll have acquired all the knowledge to go buy a business, and do it right."

I was taken aback. I hadn't had a "job" in decades. But the idea resonated with me. And it took me back to the story of *The King's Flyswatter*.

As I evaluated the small plumbing and HVAC business, I felt like Ubar trying to dive headfirst into the rope business. What kind of idiot would buy a plumbing and HVAC business without knowing what they don't know? I needed to swat flies again, to learn this business from the ground up. And what better opportunity could there be than in the rapidly growing Goettl organization. Ken and I agreed to think it over, and I spent the next week fleshing out the idea and discussing it with my wife.

Then I accepted the offer and got to work.

Back to Flyswatting

I spent several months gaining access to the business and finding out everything I could about the operation and being part of management meetings, even before I drew my first paycheck. When the time was right, I was added to the payroll and was once again a W-2 employee. I was trained as a general manager, and when the company acquired a business in Austin, Texas, a few months later, they asked me to run it.

My task was to integrate it into the systems and processes that we operated and make it part of the Goettl platform. So I was once again swatting flies, both doing the job that I was asked to do and learning a thousand other things I'd need to know to own a business of this type.

About a year later, I'd wrapped up the integration and trained my replacement. Meanwhile, the entire company was acquired in a much-celebrated transaction. I was asked to take on one more task: to handle change management at an existing branch. I would spend six more months facing new challenges and learning yet another set of skills.

As I write this book, I am at the end of my time at Goettl. The business is flourishing. The branches where I worked are hitting their stride. I have poured my blood, sweat, and tears into the work, and, I believe, delivered over and above what was expected. It's been a satisfying journey.

Even so, I find myself standing at a crossroad similar to the one I faced in my very first job as a lawyer twenty years ago. I can stay, continue to grow here and be part of something bigger. Or I can take this opportunity to step into a new chapter. Perhaps I could buy a company of my own. I'm certainly in a much better position to do that now. I have other business investments as well and plenty of opportunity for more. I don't feel the need to stay in the HVAC business or, indeed, in any particular industry.

I realize many people in this position would choose to stay, and there's absolutely nothing wrong with that. Like Ubar, when offered a position in the palace of the new king, I understand that I could have a rewarding and comfortable life here.

But I follow the Way of the Flyswatter. I am always learning, always a bit restless for the next opportunity, even when I'm not entirely sure what it will be. I can leave with confidence, because I am Ubar. I have acquired a vast treasure of knowledge, skills, and competence, as well as a network, a good reputation, and the spoils of success.

Don't Get Stuck Swatting Flies

If someone is merely a flyswatter, they are forever stuck swatting flies. They live in fear of losing their jobs, and when they finally get fed up and make a change, they usually wind up doing the same work elsewhere. As Andrew Wilkinson put it, "Most successful people are just an anxiety disorder harnessed for productivity."[5] That's no life for me. And I suspect it's no life for you, either.

The decision to leave a highly paid, enviable job with a

fast growing company is an easy one for me. I don't say that to humble brag about my success, but to show you that *The King's Flyswatter* is a true story, in the sense that it illustrates principles that hold up well in business and in life. My journey, and that of many others, is proof. I am Ubar.

I have taken every job experience in my life as an opportunity to gain skills and knowledge. Those skills and knowledge have become assets that cannot be taken away. I have built a network and a reputation with intention. I have ventured and failed, but each failure left me richer in wisdom—even if lighter in the purse. That richness in knowledge and relationships has given me one of the only freedoms available to us in this modern, capitalist world—the freedom to choose whether to stay or go.

As a simple wage earner, I would lack that freedom. The golden handcuffs of inner anxiety and modest gain would hold me in place. As a free agent, rich with wisdom, skill, and relationships, I am free both to stay where I am and to go out on my own.

I am very appreciative of Ken Goodrich and many others in the Goettl organization. Yet I am sure that if I were to stay, there would soon be a day when I walked up to the front door and, like my friend Cory, could not bear to open it and go in. Leaving now will preserve what I've invested in: my reputation, my relationship capital, and a legacy of mentoring and growing others who have been under my leadership.

This same freedom can be yours. If you are tired of doing

work you despise and feeling stuck in your golden handcuffs, they can be removed. You are Ubar, too.

Wherever you are along this path, you are now on a journey toward something most "wage earners" will never have: autonomy. You are working toward having more agency; the freedom to stay and grow in a company, or to leave and start your own thing. Learn a job besides your own. Acquire abilities you do not yet have. Make relationships with people who are further along on the journey than you are. Develop your superpower.

To move from employee to owner, you really only need two things: competence and connection. Both are available to you right now, right here, wherever you happen to be. That is the Way of the Flyswatter. It worked for Ubar, it worked for me, and it'll work for you.

Flyswatting in Action

There is nothing wrong with going back to swatting flies. Every season brings with it new opportunities and challenges, and there may come a time after you've gone off on your own when you have a chance to work for someone else again. If the benefits outweigh the cost, take it.

Always do more than what is required of you, and you will always have options. Learners need not fear change and should embrace it as opportunity. Don't get stuck merely swatting flies when what you're really after is learning new skills. You can build skills and develop a network right now, in whatever your current situation happens to be.

When the time comes for you to move on, trust the Way of the Flyswatter. There is always someone else to help, something new to learn, some new challenge to teach you.

POSTLUDE

It is I, Sabium, Divine Emperor of Babylon, Sumeria, Akkadia, and the all lands of Anu, who write this story.

My grandfather was the Divine Tattannu, King of Namir. My father was Abdili the Great, who expanded the kingdom of Namir to create the greatest kingdom of the east, Babylon. Many years have passed since the reign of my grandfather, Tattannu, and many more since my own father, Abdili, entered the presence of Anu.

During his lifetime, my father taught me the wisdom he had learned at the feet of the humble flyswatter known as Ubar. I attest that all these things are true and trustworthy. The empire has prospered greatly from the teaching of Ubar. The Way of the Flyswatter is taught to every young child, from least to greatest.

As for Ubar, who served both my father and grandfather, he became the most prosperous of all cattle breeders, supplying an abundance of meat and milk to our growing kingdom. In all of Babylon, there has never been a wiser man than Ubar, the King's Flyswatter. For he taught both servant and king the way to freedom. What you desire, you can achieve if you are willing to take responsibility for yourself, learn all that you can no matter how lowly your position, and put your well-laid plans into action. This is the Way of the Flyswatter.

WHY NOT YOU?

It was Happy Hour in San Diego. I was sitting at a bar with Brian Karscig from the band Louis XIV, enjoying a lazy afternoon and talking about music, business, and all things in between. Brian is an entrepreneur in several ways, including as a pioneering musician and successful record producer. He's also cofounder of a music software venture. Most people look at a guy like Brian and chalk all that up to raw talent. Sure, he's successful. He's a killer guitarist and a great songwriter. In fact, he has toured with the Killers as a guitarist. Why wouldn't he rise to the top?

Talent matters, of course, and Brian's work ethic is second to none. But that's not what sets him apart from so many would-be artists and producers vying for success in the music business. There's one thing more.

As we sat sipping sangrias, a musician came into the room and began to set up his mic and guitar to play a set.

Brian recognized the guy and waved him over to the table. They knew each other, which is not surprising in San Diego. It's a small town in many ways, even smaller in the music business. They chatted for a minute, then Brian took a seat and the singer got up to play.

Within a few minutes, I began to think, "This guy is *really* good." He was laying down an incredible set, covering a wide variety of popular songs. I was surprised to see him playing Happy Hour on a Thursday afternoon. So I asked Brian, "Why do you think this guy hasn't broken out of the lounge circuit? He's got the talent."

"You're right," Brian said. "This guy is good. Way more talented than I am."

"Okay," I said, "but that doesn't explain why he's up there while you're recording chart-topping hits and touring the world. How does that happen?"

Brian thought for a minute while we listened to the music. Then he gave a really simple answer. He said, "I just believed I could, and I had nothing to lose by trying."

I hadn't seen that coming, but I knew immediately that it was true. It's the same answer I'd have given if he'd asked me the same question.

What keeps talented lawyers slaving away in law offices while people like me head out the door and start their own firm? Was I more talented? No. Was I smarter? Nope. Lucky? Not really. But I believed I could do it, and I knew nothing would happen until I took action to make it happen.

There are certainly many factors in success. Malcolm Gladwell points out the success of those who have ten thousand hours of practice, like Bill Gates and the Beatles. Practice long enough, gain enough skill, and your success will be automatic, so it seems.

Frank Partnoy, one of my law professors, talks about delay as a vital part of most success stories[6]. Bide your time. Look for the golden opportunity. Wait for the right moment. Launch too soon and you'll fail. Delay just long enough and success is all but guaranteed. We focus too much on the high profile gurus of business, the unicorns and the origins of meme-stock companies.

Indeed, the stories of business icons are inspiring. But notice how they actually inhibit us from pursuing our goals. Rather than filling us with a sense of empowerment, these inspirational tales keep us slaving away at our desks. We can't step out and try because we haven't had a stroke of genius, or we don't have ten thousand hours of practice, or we haven't waited long enough, or paid our dues, or saved enough money, or whatever else the success gurus say is necessary.

So we wait, and wait, and wait. Until one day we realize we're closer to the end than the beginning, and we're still playing guitar at Happy Hour, or grinding out billable hours, or punching the clock at a business we don't own.

So the real question we need to ask ourselves is not, "Do I have enough experience?" or, "Am I the most talented person I know?" The answer to both questions is almost certainly no.

The real question to ask is one like Brian Karscig asked himself all those years ago, the question I asked myself at the very beginning of my journey: "Why not me?"

There is no box you can check that says, "I am fully ready to make the leap." If you start making a list of all the things that have to happen before you make your move, you'll be a list maker for the rest of your life. Listen to this, because it's the most important message in this book and I have a feeling that you need to hear it:

You are enough.

You have as much talent as you need.

You can do this thing as well as anyone else.

So do it.

Or you can play the perfect set at Happy Hour every Thursday afternoon for the rest of your life.

Many people with greater skill than you have remained stuck in a job they hate, working for people they dislike, never gathering the courage to break free. And people of far lesser skill have followed their dream, found the meaningful work they crave, and have made millions, even billions, in the process.

Why not you?

ACKNOWLEDGMENTS

First, I'd like to thank my wonderful wife who put up with me writing when I should have been relaxing on a trip or spending time with her on that trip. She has been the center of my journey, a partner in most ventures as well as in all of life. She is my foundation, coconspirator, business partner, collaborator, and thankfully a fan of my thinking and writing, a supporter in every sense of the word.

I could not have brought this book to fruition without my writing coach Jeff Goins and his team at Fresh Complaint who embraced the concept of an ancient parable with modern-day application and helped bring it to life. Thank you, Jeff, for also helping me see how my personal story could be crafted to illuminate this fable. I'm grateful to Larry Wilson for the hard work of putting the pieces together and seeing the project through to completion. Also, thank you to Kirstyn Smith for her editorial help and to Sandy Kreps for all the behind-the-scenes project management wizardry.

I use my best friend and business partner Cory Verner as an example of what not to do in the beginning not because he made a mistake, but because his story resonates with so many people who feel stuck at a job they hate. He really has been a flyswatter, learning business when he was in college painting houses and later learning sales and home services while working for a pest control company. He left his job in haste, but with a large reserve of capital, a network of relationships, and a side gig that utilized the skills from his former employer to work for himself. I appreciate his work on the audiobook, in addition to being one of the star figures in the book. Currently, we are cofounders of multiple ventures in the audiobook publishing world, where we're applying 20 years of experience swatting flies in that industry.

I also have to thank Kayla for being *my* flyswatter for so many years and for being the one to take over my law practice when the time came. Kayla has empowered me to move onward, burn the boats, and go all in on myself as an entrepreneur.

In addition, I want to acknowledge so many people who have helped me achieve my goals and been part of my flyswatter journey. The list could fill many pages, but to name a few: I'm thankful for the opportunity to clean toilets (and learn property management) from Tom Heatherington and Darlene Allen. I'm equally grateful to my legal mentors Whitney Their and Ted Quirk. And I want to acknowledge Ken Goodrich and the executive team that embraced me at

Goettl—Darin Wetzler, Dave Wick, Jason Ross, and Rohin Lal—and the amazing team at Goettl Austin.

I dedicated this book to my friend Joshua Mitchell, because he is a shining example of someone who has walked the path of the flyswatter. My early discussions with him helped me see the pattern more clearly and bring some of these ideas to life in my Linkedin Learning course *Employee to Entrepreneur.* I'm incredibly proud of Joshua and grateful to be a part of his journey and that he has been part of mine.

I have also had the privilege of bringing many of my ideas to the world through teaching courses on Linkedin Learning (formerly Lynda.com). I am ever so grateful to Jolie Miller for her belief in me, and for giving me the platform to share my expertise.

What a privilege to have a foreword by Pat Flynn! Thank you, Pat, for your support and kind words. It is an honor to have someone I have followed and respect so much endorse my work.

Lastly, thank you to Allan Nygren and Abigail Taylor at Printopya for the help in designing and publishing this book. Your creative prowess and patience is beyond appreciated.

ENDNOTES

1 | Quentin Fottrell, "'I missed the bus on Bitcoin, but now feel like my time has come. I have another 25 years of a boring 9-to-5 job.' Is the crypto crash an opportunity to buy low?" *The Moneyist* (blog), *MarketWatch*, June 13, 2022, https://www.marketwatch.com/story/i-missed-the-bus-on-bitcoin-but-now-feel-like-my-time-has-come-is-it-time-to-go-big-or-go-home-i-have-another-25-years-of-a-boring-9-to-5-job-and-i-just-want-out-11655138006?

2 | Seth Godin, *Stop Stealing Dreams (What is school for?)*, (self-pub., Do You Zoom, Inc., 2012), PDF.

3 | Carol Hodanbosi, "The First and Second Laws of Motion," *NASA*, updated May 13, 2021, https://www.grc.nasa.gov/www/k-12/WindTunnel/Activities/first2nd_lawsf_motion.html

4 | Although I note that many companies promote based on the Peter Principle, where employees are promoted to the point of incompetence. This is another reason many ambitious employees (like you) want to move from being at the whim of an incompetent manager to being self-employed, and having personal and professional freedom. See, *The Peter Principle* (William Morrow and Company) by Laurence Peter and Raymond Hull (1969).

5 | Andrew Wilkinson (@awilkinson), Twitter, April 26, 2021, 10:07 a.m., https://twitter.com/awilkinson/status/1386698431905730565?lang=en

6 | Frank Partnoy, *Wait: The Art and Science of Delay* (New York: Public Affairs, 2012).